D0041971

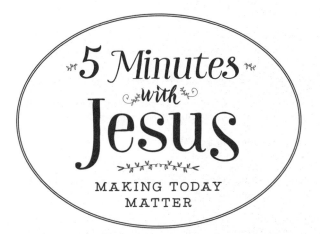

5 Minutes with Jesus

with

Jesus

MAKING TODAY
MATTER

Sheila Walsh

THOMAS NELSON
Since 1798

NASHVILLE   MEXICO CITY   RIO DE JANEIRO

Published in Nashville, Tennessee, by Thomas Nelson. Thomas Nelson is a registered trademark of HarperCollins Christian Publishing, Inc.

Cover design by Katie Jennings Design

Unless otherwise noted, Scripture quotations are taken from *Holy Bible*, New Living Translation. © 1996. Used by permission of Tyndale House Publishers, Inc., Wheaton, Illinois 60189. All rights reserved.

Scripture quotations marked MSG are taken from *The Message* by Eugene H. Peterson. © 1993, 1994, 1995, 1996, 2000. Used by permission of NavPress Publishing Group. All rights reserved. HCSB from *Holman Christian Standard Bible*. © 1999, 2000, 2002, 2003 by Broadman and Holman Publishers. All rights reserved. NASB from the NEW AMERICAN STANDARD BIBLE®, © The Lockman Foundation 1960, 1962, 1963, 1968, 1971, 1972, 1973, 1975, 1977, 1995. Used by permission. NIV from the Holy Bible, New International Version®, NIV®. Copyright © 1973, 1978, 1984, 2011 by Biblica, Inc.™ Used by permission of Zondervan. All rights reserved worldwide. *www.zondervan.com*. NKJV from THE NEW KING JAMES VERSION. © 1982 by Thomas Nelson, Inc. Used by permission. All rights reserved. ESV from THE ENGLISH STANDARD VERSION. © 2001 by Crossway Bibles, a division of Good News Publishers. *The Voice* from *The Voice*. © 2008 and 2009 Ecclesia Bible Society. Used by permission. All rights reserved.

ISBN: 978-0-7180-3253-1

Printed in the United States of America

15 16 17 18 19 DCI 6 5 4 3 2

Introduction: Life-Changing Truths for Your Full and Fast-Paced Days

I don't know where you are in your journey, but I know this: you are busy. You have a list of twenty-five things to do and time to do about five of them . . . on a good day! I get that. I know what it's like to rush out the door, mentally ticking off a long "to do" list, hoping your shoes match, sloshing coffee in your to-go mug, and praying the yogurt in your purse doesn't explode. Exercise? Quiet time? Prayer? How do we fit all of that into our hectic and overwhelming lives?

That's a challenge I face just like you do. How can we walk through the just-described craziness with Jesus? I know it seems like we really don't have time for *one more thing*. But I also know that God's time is not like ours, and when we give Him our time, He can do more within us in five minutes than if we spent five hours on our own. Jesus said He came that we might have life to the full—and I'm sure He was talking about a different kind of full than what most of us are currently experiencing! But the good news is, just like a moment with the Savior transformed countless lives when He walked on the earth, a moment with Him today can transform us. Yet I often go about my busy day, completely forgetting that peace, perspective, and grace are right within my grasp.

I hope both you and I will learn to find a few quiet minutes each day when we can listen for God to speak to us through His Word. I hope we'll read the Bible and slowly absorb the words that are meant to bring us life. And in those precious moments, I pray that we will begin a conversation with Jesus that we will continue throughout that day—a conversation that Jesus will use to encourage, guide, and strengthen us. And over time may we find these day-long conversations giving us great peace despite the chaos of life.

It is the desire of my heart that on each page you'll find truth from God's Word that will nourish you, sustain you, and remind you that you are not alone. That's the joy of the body of Christ: we get to do life together. I would love to hear how spending five minutes with Jesus is changing your life!

Noise Pollution

S top for a moment and just listen. What do you hear? Maybe the neighbor's lawnmower . . . the barking dog a few houses down . . . a clock ticking . . . the cars on the street.

Now stop for a moment and just listen to the noise *inside*. What is keeping your heart from being quiet and at peace? Most likely, it's many things, because although we long for peace, real life intrudes.

A call from the doctor

A note from the teacher about a child's behavior

A lost job and a pile of bills

Real life does not foster internal peace!

In the last major conversation Jesus had with His closest friends, He spoke about peace—but not as we might have expected Him to. When I read Jesus saying, "I've told you all this so that you may have peace" (John 16:33), my first question is *All what*? If I didn't look back to John 15 to see what Jesus had been saying, I'd guess that keys to peace would be something along these lines:

"You're going to live to a ripe old age."

"Your children will rise up and call you blessed—even when they hit fifteen."

"You will always have enough money for all you need and most of what you want."

"You will hear the Lord tell you 'Well done' after a lifetime of faithfulness."

Sounds good, right? But not one of these things was included in the strangest "peace speech" I've ever read. Turn to John 15 and you'll see that Jesus told His closest friends that they would be persecuted and no longer welcome in places they used to go. Go to John 16:2 and you'll find these devastating words: "You will be expelled from the synagogues, and the time is coming when those who kill you will think they are doing a holy service for God."

Clearly the peace Jesus spoke about is not what we think of at all. He was saying to His disciples—and to you and me today—"It's going to get rough down here, but don't worry. I am with you. I will never leave you. And *I* am your peace."

No matter what is going on in your life, stop for a moment and speak His name out loud: "Jesus . . . Jesus . . . Jesus." Know that He is *with* you and that He is *for* you even when the storm is raging all around.

> *Peace is not the absence of trouble;*
> *it is the presence of Christ.*

⚘ Five Minutes in the Word ⚘

"I am leaving you with a gift—peace of mind
and heart. And the peace I give is a gift the world
cannot give. So don't be troubled or afraid."
John 14:27

Those who love your instructions have
great peace and do not stumble.
Psalm 119:165

"I have told you all this so that you may have peace in me. Here on earth you will have many trials and sorrows. But take heart, because I have overcome the world."

John 16:33

In peace I will lie down and sleep, for you alone, O LORD, will keep me safe.

Psalm 4:8

For a child is born to us, a son is given to us. The government will rest on his shoulders. And he will be called: Wonderful Counselor, Mighty God, Everlasting Father, Prince of Peace. His government and its peace will never end.

Isaiah 9:6–7

Being Honest with God

"I am angry!" she said to me.

It was a strange way to start a conversation, but her emotions seemed to overwhelm her.

I had just finished teaching, and I was signing a book for someone when this woman stepped between us. Asking her to wait just a second, I finished signing the book and handed it back to the now very concerned recipient.

"Let's walk for a bit," I suggested to my unhappy new friend. When we were finally alone, I quietly asked her, "What happened to you?"

For half a second I thought she might slap me, but as I watched, the ice in her eyes melted from anger into intense pain. She fell into my arms, and rivers of tears streamed down her face.

"I've buried two sons," she said when she could speak. "Every time I hear you talk about your boy, it's like a knife in my heart."

We talked for a long time that night. At one point I asked her if she had let God see her rage, and she seemed horrified by the suggestion.

"I can't talk to God like that!" she said.

"Don't you think He already knows?" I asked, holding her tight. "He knows—and He loves you. He knows—and He wants you to trust Him enough to tell Him the whole truth about what you're feeling."

Have you ever done that? Have you ever simply gotten alone with God and let Him have it all, the good, the bad, and the downright ugly—*whatever* it is you're thinking and feeling? Doing so will change your life. Trust me; I speak from experience! But it took me years to open up to God. I'd lived much of my life filled with shame, with the profound sense that no matter what I did, I would never be good enough for God or for anyone else. Clinging to that falsehood, I kept a wall around my heart so that no one could hurt me. The wall kept me safe, but it also kept me lonely. One night when I was alone in a hospital, alone in the dark, I spoke out loud to God everything I felt. It wasn't pretty . . . but I wasn't struck by lightning. Instead I actually felt closer to Him than ever before. Truth does that. Truth destroys walls.

Are you willing to take that risk today? Will you fall at the feet of Jesus, tell Him the whole truth about what you're thinking and feeling, and then let Him love you back to life?

> *God knows your whole*
> *story and He loves you.*

⟡ Five Minutes in the Word ⟡

The Lord is close to all who call on him,
yes, to all who call on him in truth.
Psalm 145:18

"You will know the truth, and the truth will set you free."
John 8:32

Send out your light and your truth; let them guide me. Let them
lead me to your holy mountain, to the place where you live.
Psalm 43:3

Unfailing love and truth have met together. Righteousness
and peace have kissed! Truth springs up from the earth,
and righteousness smiles down from heaven.
Psalm 85:10–11

"The time is coming—indeed it's here now—when true worshipers will worship the Father in spirit and in truth. The Father is looking for those who will worship him that way."

John 4:23

Real Rest

When is the last time you felt rested? I don't mean the time you managed to get to bed before midnight. I mean really rested.

We don't live in a culture conducive to rest. Even in the church we can end up being overcommitted because we say yes too often. After all, it's easier to say no to attending a neighborhood party than to signing up for a Bible study. If something sounds spiritual, we too easily think we should line up behind everyone else and take a ticket. But being busy for God and knowing God are two different things. And often they don't fit together well.

One day when Jesus addressed a crowd, He spoke right to their bone-deep weariness: "Come to me, all of you who are weary and carry heavy burdens, and I will give you rest" (Matthew 11:28). He wasn't speaking about the kind of tiredness you and I feel at the end of a good day's work,

when we just want to sink into a chair and not move until Christmas. No, Jesus was speaking to those who were worn out trying to do the right thing to please God and earn their salvation. Remember, this was before the Crucifixion and the resurrection, so if you were a God-fearing Jew listening to Jesus that day, you still woke up every morning under the burden of 613 laws. We know the Big 10, the commandments God gave Moses on Mount Sinai, but there were 603 more for the Jewish people to follow. Add to that weight the reality that the religious leaders of the day did nothing to ease the people's burden. Jesus spoke directly to that fact:

> The teachers of religious law and the Pharisees are the official interpreters of the law of Moses. So practice and obey whatever they tell you, but don't follow their example. For they don't practice what they teach. They crush people with unbearable religious demands and never lift a finger to ease the burden. (Matthew 23:2–4)

Jesus loves you. That's the whole sentence. There's no *if* tacked on at the end. It stands alone. Jesus loves you and me just as we are right now. Despite the countless shades of light and dark that live inside us, we are loved completely by God. Hard to take in, isn't it?

That kind of love doesn't exist apart from God.

That kind of love is hard to grasp when we're busy running from one activity to another.

That kind of love calls us to rest—really rest—in the presence of the One who made us, who knows us, who loves us.

> *Real rest comes with knowing the grace of our salvation in Jesus. We don't have to earn it.*

⤷ Five Minutes in the Word ↵

Jesus said, "Come to me, all of you who are weary and carry heavy burdens, and I will give you rest. Take my yoke upon you. Let me teach you, because I am humble and gentle at heart, and you will find rest for your souls. For my yoke is easy to bear, and the burden I give you is light."
Matthew 11:28–30

*I said to myself, "Relax and rest. G*OD *has showered you with blessings. Soul, you've been rescued from death; Eye, you've been rescued from tears; and you, Foot, were kept from stumbling."*
Psalm 116:7–8 MSG

*The L*ORD *is my shepherd; I have all that I need. He lets me rest in green meadows; he leads me beside peaceful streams. He renews my strength. He guides me along right paths, bringing honor to his name.*
Psalm 23:1–3

I see that the Lord is always with me. I will not be shaken, for he is right beside me. No wonder my heart is glad, and my tongue shouts his praises! My body rests in hope.
Acts 2:25–26

Those who live in the shelter of the Most High will find rest in the shadow of the Almighty.
Psalm 91:1

Let Go!

I vividly remember one Sunday afternoon when Christian was three. We'd been to church and had lunch, and it was time for him to nap. I tucked him in—and not five minutes later he reappeared. I settled him again. Three minutes later he did an encore. With his fourth appearance, I'd had enough.

"Christian, I want you to lie here and ask God to help you be quiet and still." A few minutes later he popped his head into the den where I was reading a book.

"Didn't you ask God to help you?" I asked him.

"I did," he replied. "But He said that's just not how He made me!"

Perhaps that's how you feel when you read the words *Be still, and know that I am God.* I know I sometimes do. Countless times I've sat down to try to be still and holy. It's never worked very well. Only recently when I was studying this passage did I realize my misunderstanding of the text: the original Hebrew root of *Be still* doesn't mean "be

quiet"; it means "let go." That's very different, don't you think? *Let go and know that I am God!*

Let go of trying to control your spouse!

Let go of your worry about your finances!

Let go of your unforgiveness!

Let go of your past!

Let go of what you can't control—and rest in the knowledge that God is in control!

We worry so much about things that we can't impact. What if we decided to make a list of things we are holding onto and release all of them to God? What if we took one moment each day to be still and acknowledge God's perfect control? Let's give it a try.

> *"Let go and know that I am God."*

✦ Five Minutes in the Word ✦

Be still, and know that I am God. I will be exalted among the nations, I will be exalted in the earth!
Psalm 46:10 ESV

Do you know how God controls the storm and causes the lightning to flash from his clouds? Do you understand how he moves the clouds with wonderful perfection and skill? When you are sweltering in your clothes and the south wind dies down and everything is still, he makes the skies reflect the heat like a bronze mirror. Can you do that?

Job 37:15–18

Yours, O LORD, is the greatness and the power and the glory and the victory and the majesty, for all that is in the heavens and in the earth is yours. Yours is the kingdom, O LORD, and you are exalted as head above all. Both riches and honor come from you, and you rule over all. In your hand are power and might, and in your hand it is to make great and to give strength to all.

1 Chronicles 29:11–12 ESV

Remember the things I have done in the past. For I alone am God! I am God, and there is none like me. Only I can tell you the future before it even happens. Everything I plan will come to pass, for I do whatever I wish.

Isaiah 46:9–10

Your Unique Purpose

When I was sixteen, I had a summer job working at Houston's, the only department store in my Scottish hometown of Ayr. I was assigned the *haberdashery*—and I had no idea what that even was. My new boss told me that we specialized in "small articles for sewing, such as buttons, ribbons, zips, and other notions," and I didn't dare ask what "notions" were!

My first task was sorting and rewinding ribbon spools. Then I reorganized the behind-the-counter drawers. All went well until I encountered *it*—and suddenly I was beyond confused. *Why would that be here and not in the hardware department?*

When I showed my boss the pristine drawers, she seemed suitably impressed. "But that thingy in the bottom drawer—should I leave it there or take it somewhere else?" I asked.

"Just leave it there," she said. "We had quite a rush on those with young girls this summer!"

"Girls bought those?" I said. "I don't think I'll *ever* be buying one."

"Every girl says that until she meets the right one," my boss said with a smile.

"Why would I ever need a plunger with a lacy handle?" Yes, I asked that question out loud—and I kept talking. "The first time you use it, you'd ruin the lace."

I discovered that day—much to the delight of the entire staff of eyewitnesses to my ignorance—that that strange object was actually a form for a bride's bouquet. They'd put flowers on it and carry it by the decorated handle. Who knew!

Not knowing the purpose of a lacy plunger is hardly as critical as not knowing our purpose on this planet. You and I are not randomly placed in just any home. You and I are chosen daughters of the Most High God, and each of us has a divine plan and purpose to fulfill. At times we lose that big-picture perspective. After all, we're busy with our families and our other tasks, but our busyness does not and cannot alter our sovereign God's plan for our lives. If you doubt that statement, read this:

You watched me as I was being formed in utter seclusion,
as I was woven together in the dark of the womb.
You saw me before I was born.
Every day of my life was recorded in your book.
Every moment was laid out
before a single day had passed. (Psalm 139:15–16)

God has a unique purpose for you and you alone. Look to Him to guide you. Stay focused on Him and, as a result, mindful of that purpose. And remember that while you and I tend to look at externals and compare ourselves to others, God looks at the heart, and He also speaks to our hearts. So, if you're not sure, ask God to show you why He made you. Ask Him to reveal *to* you His specific purpose *for* you!

Who knows whether you have come to this particular place for such a time as this?

✎ Five Minutes in the Word ✎

Your word is a lamp to my feet and a light to my path.
Psalm 119:105 ESV

Do you not know that your body is a temple of the Holy Spirit within you, whom you have from God? You are not your own, for you were bought with a price. So glorify God in your body.
1 Corinthians 6:19–20 ESV

I cry out to God Most High, to God who fulfills his purpose for me.
Psalm 57:2 ESV

"I know the plans I have for you," declares the Lord, "plans to prosper you and not to harm you, plans to give you hope and a future. Then you will call on me and come and pray to me, and I will listen to you. You will seek me and find me when you seek me with all your heart."
Jeremiah 29:11–13 NIV

A Living Sacrifice

Parents with older children had warned me about this project, the crowning glory of seventh grade, but I still wasn't prepared for how much work it involved. Each student had to build a to-scale model of the tabernacle of the Lord as outlined in Exodus 36–39. Have you ever read a detailed account of the tabernacle? It is incredibly intricate. It makes the Taj Mahal look thrown together.

We visited several craft shops, and then Christian got to work. His greatest challenge was the to-scale part. After his first noble attempt, I asked him, "Do you see any kind of problem with the high priest and the animal he is about to sacrifice?"

Christian studied the plastic figures intently. "Do you mean that the lamb is four times the size of the priest?"

"Yep, that's it," I said. "He'd need a crane to get that critter onto the altar."

We got a smaller lamb and a slightly larger priest. The

tabernacle was starting to look really good, so I left Christian to put on the finishing touches while I fixed supper. Ten minutes later he stormed into the kitchen. "I need a hot glue gun, a hammer, and a big nail!"

"Why? I thought you were finished."

"I was, but the lamb keeps falling off the altar!"

That's a problem for all of us who—to quote the apostle Paul—are *living* sacrifices. We can crawl right off the altar when it gets too hot!

And it can get pretty hot as we try to serve our family, love our neighbor, and obey God's commands. It can get hot as we try to love God with all we are and faithfully worship Jesus both when the sun shines and when the storm rages. But when we worship God, even with tear-soaked faces as the altar gets very hot, we sacrifice our desire to understand the *whys* of our life. And when we seek God's guidance and choose to obey Him, we sacrifice ourselves, dying a little more to our desire to be lord of our life.

> *Choosing to be a living sacrifice*
> *honors Jesus, the Lamb of God,*
> *who chose to be sacrificed for our sin.*

❦ Five Minutes in the Word ❧

*I appeal to you therefore, brothers, by the mercies of God,
to present your bodies as a living sacrifice, holy and
acceptable to God, which is your spiritual worship. Do not be
conformed to this world, but be transformed by the renewal
of your mind, that by testing you may discern what is the
will of God, what is good and acceptable and perfect.*

Romans 12:1–2 ESV

*Praise the LORD, my soul; all my inmost being, praise his
holy name. Praise the LORD, my soul, and forget not all
his benefits—who forgives all your sins and heals all your
diseases, who redeems your life from the pit and crowns you
with love and compassion, who satisfies your desires with
good things so that your youth is renewed like the eagle's.*

Psalm 103:1–5 NIV

*Since we are surrounded by such a great cloud of witnesses,
let us throw off everything that hinders and the sin that so
easily entangles. And let us run with perseverance the race*

marked out for us, fixing our eyes on Jesus, the pioneer and perfecter of faith. For the joy set before him he endured the cross, scorning its shame, and sat down at the right hand of the throne of God. Consider him who endured such opposition from sinners, so that you will not grow weary and lose heart.

Hebrews 12:1–3 NIV

Because of your unfailing love, I can enter your house; I will worship at your Temple with deepest awe.

Psalm 5:7

Offering Your Not-Enough

If my friend hadn't been the one to ask the favor, I would never have said yes. The thought of speaking to a crowd of any size terrified me. My background was singing and, later, television—speaking is another animal altogether. But my friend was desperate.

"Since my keynote speaker dropped out with the flu, I've asked every female speaker I know, and they're all booked!"

"Marlene, it's not that I'm unwilling. I just don't know how to do that," I explained. "I've never done that in my life. There *must* be someone else!"

"Trust me, I've asked everyone I can think of. You're the bottom of the barrel!"

With that rousing vote of confidence ringing in my ears, I headed to the event venue. I had pictured in my mind a casual affair with fifty or so sweet women who had very low expectations. Wrong! There were one thousand—no kidding!—beautifully coiffed and finely tailored women anticipating the motivational speech of the decade.

I stood at the podium and whispered to the Lord, "Under-catered!"

He whispered back, "What do you have?"

Let me explain our cryptic conversation. All four gospel writers include the account of Jesus feeding five thousand men—and goodness knows how many women and children—on a hillside one day, so it must be an important story. But exactly what can you and I learn from what happened as the sun began to set that day?

It was a spectacular miracle for sure, but I think there's more to it. Matthew reported that Jesus told the disciples to feed the people. Luke mentioned Jesus' instructions to arrange the crowd into groups of fifty. According to John, Jesus asked Phillip where they could buy enough bread to feed the crowd. Only Mark included this significant question that came from Jesus' lips: "How much bread do you have?"

All that the disciples could see was what they *needed*; they missed seeing what they *had*. Was what they had enough? No! What you and I have is never enough. But when we give what we have to Jesus, He blesses it, breaks it, and feeds His people.

One more thing: Do you think the only person on the hillside that day with food was the little boy with his packed lunch? Of course not! There were moms and grandmas, and where there are women, there are snacks. Maybe no one else offered the food they had because they knew it wouldn't be enough for the thousands gathered.

Look at your life right now. What can you take to Jesus? Do you hesitate because it's not as much as someone else can give? Are you embarrassed because it can't possibly be enough to accomplish the task? Hear this: Christ never expects us to bring what is needed. He asks us to give Him what we have, and He makes it work—often with leftovers.

> *When you add your not-enough to Christ's more-than-enough, miracles happen.*

ꙮ Five Minutes in the Word ꙮ

[Jesus] said to [His disciples], "How many loaves do you have?"
Mark 6:38 ESV

It is not that we think we are qualified to do anything on our own. Our qualification comes from God. He has enabled us to be ministers of his new covenant. This is a covenant not of written laws, but of the Spirit.
2 Corinthians 3:5–6

*I know how to live on almost nothing or with everything. I
have learned the secret of living in every situation, whether
it is with a full stomach or empty, with plenty or little. For I
can do everything through Christ, who gives me strength.*
Philippians 4:12–13

*Remember, dear brothers and sisters, that few of you were wise
in the world's eyes or powerful or wealthy when God called you.
Instead, God chose things the world considers foolish in order to
shame those who think they are wise. And he chose things that
are powerless to shame those who are powerful. God chose things
despised by the world, things counted as nothing at all, and used
them to bring to nothing what the world considers important.
As a result, no one can ever boast in the presence of God.*
1 Corinthians 1:26–29

*Whatever you do, work at it with all your heart, as
working for the Lord, not for human masters, since you
know that you will receive an inheritance from the Lord
as a reward. It is the Lord Christ you are serving.*
Colossians 3:23–24 NIV

God's Antidote to Shame

I t was a setup.

My New Testament professor confessed to it after the laughter died down. "One student falls for that every year!" he said, clearly satisfied that I'd taken the bait.

I don't even remember the question. It was something about how the writers of the Old and New Testaments were inspired. Did they hear God's voice? Did they sit with pen in hand as the Holy Spirit dictated to them?

While I don't remember the exact question, I remember all too well how I felt as everyone around me laughed. I pretended to laugh, too, but the smile went no deeper than my face. Inside I felt a familiar desire to crawl into a corner by myself: I felt ashamed. And shame can kill your spirit.

Guilt tells us that we've *done* something wrong; shame tells us that we *are* something wrong. If we've done something wrong, we can try to make it right, but what do we do if we feel at our very core that we *are* wrong?

The more I study and apply the Word of God to my life, the more clearly I see—from Genesis to Revelation—that God's antidote to shame is His love. We see God administer this antidote from the moment Adam and Eve fell from grace and shame entered the world, through the ages, up to the Lamb of God on Golgotha's brutal stage crying, "It is finished."

Shame tells us we are worthless. Christ says, "I have made you worthy."

Shame tells us we don't belong. Christ says, "You are Mine."

Shame tells us we are dirty. Christ says, "I will wash you as white as snow."

I invite you to take a few moments to do something that has helped me: write down those life experiences that have caused you to feel shame. Then for each item you listed, hear Jesus speak His words of love over you.

> *God's love is the antidote to shame.*

⋙ Five Minutes in the Word ⋘

Now the man and his wife were both
naked, but they felt no shame.

Genesis 2:25

At that moment their eyes were opened, and they
suddenly felt shame at their nakedness.

Genesis 3:7

To you they cried out and were rescued;
in you they trusted and were not put to shame.

Psalm 22:5 ESV

See, I lay a stone in Zion, a chosen and precious cornerstone,
and the one who trusts in him will never be put to shame.

1 Peter 2:6 NIV

"Come now, let us settle the matter," says the LORD. "Though
your sins are like scarlet, they shall be as white as snow;
though they are red as crimson, they shall be like wool."

Isaiah 1:18 NIV

The Power of Forgiveness

Science fascinates my son. I've seen this passion in Christian since he was a child. In fact, during his pursuit of this passion, we've had many experiments go spectacularly wrong in our kitchen. One such experiment involved adding a small amount of one seemingly innocuous liquid to another.

"Watch this, Mom!" he said with the intensity of a young Einstein. "As the liquids meet, they'll bubble and turn into a new color."

Well, they met—and *bubble* would not quite describe what they did that day. What looked like hot-pink lava exploded out of the beaker from his Young Scientist Kit and all over the kitchen table.

"That did a lot more than I expected," he calmly said, master of the understatement.

Forgiveness is like that powerful concoction. When we begin to grasp the power of dragging our will into line

with the will of God and choosing to forgive, a lot more will happen than we expect.

We live in a world where terrible things happen to good people. I read your letters, Facebook posts, and Twitter messages every day, and every day my heart breaks a little.

The woman whose husband walks out on her

The man who is skipped over for the promised promotion

The so-called friend who lies about you and damages your reputation

The child who blames the divorce on a parent who didn't want it either

The list is endless.

We live in a very unfair world, so what are we to do? Well, I've come to understand two important things about forgiveness as I've studied God's Word. First, forgiveness is not a suggestion; it's a command. Second, it seems to me that forgiveness is God's secret weapon. Forgiveness doesn't minimize the pain, it doesn't say that what happened to you or me is okay, and it doesn't mean we have to let it happen to us again. No! What forgiveness does is either keep us from picking up a burden of anger, resentment, and bitterness—or free us from that burden if we are already carrying it. When by God's grace we forgive, we leave that weight at the foot of the cross.

Sound good? So where do we start? We start wherever we are right now. We ask the Holy Spirit to bring to mind any wounds we have buried deep, and when He does, we lay those—as well as the more obvious wrongs done against us that we need to forgive—at the foot of Jesus' cross. I also find it helpful to write down the names of people I need to forgive and burn that piece of paper. You can do this over and over and over if you need to. A lot more will happen than you thought.

Fair doesn't live in this world, but Jesus does.

Five Minutes in the Word

Bring joy to your servant, Lord, for I put my trust in you. You, Lord, are forgiving and good, abounding in love to all who call to you. Hear my prayer, LORD; listen to my cry for mercy.
Psalm 86:4–6 NIV

Love prospers when a fault is forgiven, but dwelling on it separates close friends.
Proverbs 17:9

"Give us today the food we need, and forgive us our sins, as we have forgiven those who sin against us."

Matthew 6:11–12

"Do not judge others, and you will not be judged. Do not condemn others, or it will all come back against you. Forgive others, and you will be forgiven."

Luke 6:37

Our Risen Hope

"If this is one of God's games, I don't want to play anymore," she said.

"You think God plays games with us?" I asked.

"I fought long and hard to survive breast cancer. I trusted God all the way through, and now it's back. And I'm done."

I bumped into her at one of my favorite coffee spots. She introduced herself as someone who'd heard me speak a couple of years previously, and she asked if I had time for coffee. We talked for a long time that day. I asked if I could pray for her before she left, and she politely declined. "What would be the point?"

I watched as she slipped out the door and stepped into the rain. I prayed for her anyway. I prayed for her to find hope.

It's a terrible thing to lose hope. Some of us are there right now. Some of us have broken bodies; some, broken

hearts. And others of us never imagined we'd be in a place like this—doubting, struggling, wondering why God seems to have stopped listening to us and stopped loving us.

I've been reading through Matthew's gospel, and this morning I came to this:

> When Judas, who had betrayed [Jesus], saw that Jesus was condemned, he was seized with remorse and returned the thirty pieces of silver to the chief priests and the elders. "I have sinned," he said, "for I have betrayed innocent blood."
>
> "What is that to us?" they replied. "That's your responsibility."
>
> So Judas threw the money into the temple and left. Then he went away and hanged himself. (Matthew 27:3–5 NIV)

Oh, Judas, if only you could have waited for three more days! Yes, you would have been in agony on Friday, but on Sunday morning you would have seen hope rise from the dead!

I don't know what you face right now, friend, but I do know that while we may lose a few battles on this earth, we will—because of Jesus—win the war. Don't despair!

> *On Sunday morning*
> *Hope rose from the dead.*

∽☾ Five Minutes in the Word ☽∽

Praise be to the God and Father of our Lord Jesus Christ! In his great mercy he has given us new birth into a living hope through the resurrection of Jesus Christ from the dead.

1 Peter 1:3 NIV

Lead me by your truth and teach me, for you are the God who saves me. All day long I put my hope in you.

Psalm 25:5

O Lord, you alone are my hope. I've trusted you, O LORD, from childhood. Yes, you have been with me from birth; from my mother's womb you have cared for me. No wonder I am always praising you!

Psalm 71:5–6

We believers also groan, even though we have the Holy Spirit within us as a foretaste of future glory, for we long for our bodies to be released from sin and suffering. We, too, wait with eager hope for the day when God will give us our full rights as his adopted children, including the new bodies he has promised us.

Romans 8:23

If our hope in Christ is only for this life, we are more to be pitied than anyone in the world. But in fact, Christ has been raised from the dead. He is the first of a great harvest of all who have died.

1 Corinthians 15:19–20

Let us hold tightly without wavering to the hope we affirm, for God can be trusted to keep his promise.

Hebrews 10:23

A Lesson in Perseverance . . . from a Yorkie

It had been a long weekend of delayed flights and short nights. I had finally gotten home, but Monday morning I could barely crawl out of bed. I think I was sleepwalking when I made myself a cup of coffee and headed out to the back patio with my three little dogs. And our ritual began.

Maggie the Yorkie wanted to play. She dug through her toy box until she found her stuffed raccoon. She dropped it at my feet and looked up. I didn't respond. She picked it up again, backed up a few steps, and then approached me a second time. Still nothing from me . . . because I had nothing to give! After two more futile attempts, Maggie changed her strategy and began to paw my leg. That worked. Wanting peace, I picked up the

raccoon, threw it as far as I could across the yard, and watched her run like the wind.

I want you to pray like that.

It wasn't audible, but I clearly recognized God's voice deep in my spirit. I thought about Maggie's persistence. She was totally committed to getting the answer from me that she wanted. She wasn't going to quit until I picked up her toy and threw it for her. I realized that, when it comes to praying, I often don't have a fraction of this Yorkie's perseverance. Oh, I'll pray about a situation for a while, but I'll move on.

I thought of the look in Maggie's eyes, though. She loves me, and she knows that I love her. Because of that love, she absolutely believes that if she asks long enough, I'll answer. How much more does our Father in heaven love us and want to answer us!

Jesus told the story of the persistent widow (Luke 18:1–8) to encourage us to keep dragging our prayers before God, to approach Him over and over again. With that in mind, I decided I wasn't about to be outdone by a Yorkie!

> *The Lord rejoices over a believer who loves big enough and long enough to pray until He answers.*

✽ Five Minutes in the Word ✽

*One day Jesus told his disciples a story to show that
they should always pray and never give up.*
Luke 18:1

*"When you pray, go away by yourself, shut the door
behind you, and pray to your Father in private. Then
your Father, who sees everything, will reward you."*
Matthew 6:6

*Ask in faith without doubting. For the doubter is like
the surging sea, driven and tossed by the wind.*
James 1:6 HCSB

*Pray always. Pray in the Spirit. Pray about everything in
every way you know how! And keeping all this in mind,
pray on behalf of God's people. Keep on praying feverishly,
and be on the lookout until evil has been stayed.*
Ephesians 6:18 *The Voice*

*Rejoice always; pray without ceasing; in everything give
thanks; for this is God's will for you in Christ Jesus.*
1 Thessalonians 5:16–18 NASB

Worshipping in the Dark

W hy would God give me a miracle only to snatch it away?" she cried.

It wasn't a question, really; it was a wail.

She had asked if she could talk to me for a few minutes in private during the lunch break of a conference where I was teaching.

"We were told we couldn't have children," she began. "We tried for years and years, and we'd almost given up when I discovered I was pregnant."

Light flickered for a moment in her eyes and was quickly extinguished. "He lived for four hours," she said. "Why would God do that? Why would He give me a miracle only to snatch him away?"

There was nothing I could say. Sometimes the well of human suffering is too deep for words. All I could do was hold her for a while. I prayed for her before she got up to leave—and I prayed to Someone who understands what it's like to watch a Son die. Once more I found myself drawn back to a little verse in Luke's gospel. It's a verse that's often overlooked, but I think God has tucked a tiny puzzle piece into nine words: "Blessed is the one who is not offended by me" (Luke 7:23 ESV).

You may remember the story that precedes these nine words. John the Baptist is being held in the dungeon of King Herod's palace. This man of the wilderness is confined to a dismal, dank cellar. As if that isn't painful enough, John is tormented by doubt. So tormented that he asks his friends to go to Jesus and ask Him this strange question: "Are you the one who is to come, or shall we look for another?" (Luke 7:19 ESV).

Why is this question strange? Because John had spent his whole life preparing for the moment when God would reveal the Messiah and he would have the joy of crying out, "Behold, the Lamb of God, who takes away the sin of the world!" (John 1:29 ESV). John watched that day when the Holy Spirit descended on Jesus like a dove, and John heard the voice of God declare, "This is my beloved Son" (Matthew 3:17 ESV).

But now John was in a dark prison, and doubts and lies slithered around his cell: *What if you got it all wrong, John? What if you identified the wrong man? Besides, where is Jesus now?*

Longing for an answer that would flood his cell with light, John sent his friends to Jesus. But Jesus' response was, "Tell John that I am doing the things the Messiah does," and "Blessed is the one who is not offended by me" (Luke 7:23 ESV).

In effect, Jesus was asking, "Will you love a God who's not going to get you out of that prison? Will you worship a God you don't understand? Will you still follow Me when your heart is broken?"

Times like these test our faith. Whatever dark cell you find yourself in today, will you worship God? If you choose to, He says that you are blessed.

> *God is always worthy of worship,*
> *even when we're in the dark.*

ᕄᑯ Five Minutes in the Word ᑯᕄ

[Jesus] answered [John the Baptist's disciples], "Go and tell
John what you have seen and heard: the blind receive their
sight, the lame walk, lepers are cleansed, and the deaf hear,
the dead are raised up, the poor have good news preached to
them. And blessed is the one who is not offended by me."

Luke 7:22–23 ESV

*Now faith is confidence in what we hope for and
assurance about what we do not see.*

Hebrews 11:1 NIV

*Test me, LORD, and try me, examine my heart and my
mind; for I have always been mindful of your unfailing
love and have lived in reliance on your faithfulness.*

Psalm 26:2–3 NIV

*The temptations in your life are no different from what
others experience. And God is faithful. He will not allow the
temptation to be more than you can stand. When you are
tempted, he will show you a way out so that you can endure.*

1 Corinthians 10:13

Finding Treasures
in God's Word

I love the ocean. I grew up on the west coast of Scotland by the largest and deepest coastal waters in the British Isles. I spent most of my summers exploring the rocks and caves along the coastline.

I would walk along the edge of the water with my bucket in hand and my eyes focused intently on the wet sand. And what treasures I found!

Bits of broken colored glass polished smooth by the sea and the sand

Shells of all shapes and sizes

Sneakers . . . usually just one of the pair

Legos

Rubber ducks (I still have fifteen of them)

I'd take treasures like these home, clean them off, and put them into a little brown suitcase I kept under my bed.

One day, though, I found a real treasure. I had walked the length of the shore up to the harbor wall and back to where my nana was sitting.

"Nana, can I just have five more minutes?" I asked. "I might have missed something."

"Just five minutes," she said. "It'll be getting dark soon."

I walked to the edge of the water and looked to my left, then to my right, and something sparkling in the last of the sunlight caught my eye. I bent over and saw, half-buried in the sand, a diamond engagement ring! Long story short . . . I turned it in to the police station, no one claimed the ring, it was returned to me, and I carefully placed it in the little brown suitcase beside my rubber ducks.

Now, years later, I think of that afternoon at the shore and appreciate more profoundly that God has treasures for us if we will persevere in our search. It's easy to read a few Bible verses and think we're done for the day, but we miss so much when we don't slow down, revisit our steps, and look for the treasure God always has for us in His Word.

You see, Jesus is waiting to meet us in the pages of Scripture. And His jewels of peace, grace, and love are far more valuable than anything the world can offer.

> *Slow down as you read the pages of Scripture so you don't miss any of the treasures Jesus has for you today.*

⚜ Five Minutes in the Word ⚜

Wait for the LORD; be strong, and let your heart take courage; wait for the LORD!

Psalm 27:14 ESV

Our soul waits for the LORD; he is our help and our shield. For our heart is glad in him, because we trust in his holy name.

Psalm 33:20–21 ESV

I am counting on the LORD; yes, I am counting on him. I have put my hope in his word. I long for the Lord more than sentries long for the dawn, yes, more than sentries long for the dawn.

Psalm 130:5–6

Hope that is seen is not hope. For who hopes for what he sees? But if we hope for what we do not see, we wait for it with patience. Likewise the Spirit helps us in our weakness. For we do not know what to pray for as we ought, but the Spirit himself intercedes for us with groanings too deep for words.

Romans 8:24–26 ESV

The LORD waits to be gracious to you, and therefore he exalts himself to show mercy to you. For the LORD is a God of justice; blessed are all those who wait for him.

Isaiah 30:18 ESV

Step into the Water

I remember where I was sitting when I got the news. I was at the top of the hill across from the house Barry and I were renting in Laguna Niguel, California. We climbed that hill with Bentley, our golden retriever, every morning and every evening. Barry and I had been married for a year and a half, and I was both turning forty and pregnant, so the climb took a little longer every day.

We were in a sweet place in our marriage, but financially we were bleeding to death. Barry had left one job and was looking for another, and our savings were rapidly disappearing. But a couple of weeks before this particular evening hike, I had been invited to lead worship at a new conference called Women of Faith. I was tempted to say yes because it would be regular income for at least a year, but I knew that leading worship was not my gift. So I thanked them and recommended a woman I knew.

"Lord, we're leaning on You and trusting You for what we can't see" had become our daily prayer.

Then, as the sun set over the ocean, my cell phone rang. The conversation again turned to that new conference for women, and I said, "Yes, I had a call a couple of weeks ago, but honestly, I'm not a worship leader."

"That's not why I'm calling," said the person at the other end of the line. "I want you to join the speaking team."

In one moment Barry and I went from wondering if you can reuse disposable diapers to thanking God for this beautiful far-greater-than-we-could-have-asked-or-imagined gift. It felt like we had experienced a miracle: God had opened a path through our financially impassible way just as He had opened up the Red Sea before the Israelites.

But God doesn't necessarily repeat a miracle when you find yourself at another impassible way. I write now at the end of a hard day. I've been with my Women of Faith team for eighteen years, but recently, based on the input of scripture, godly friends, and the indwelling Holy Spirit, I saw clearly that it was time to move on.

"But what's next, Lord?" I'd asked Him just this morning. "Would You show me where You want me to serve You next?"

In my spirit all I could hear was "Step into the water."

"I want to be responsible, Lord. We have bills to pay and a son about to go to college."

"Step into the water."

When the Israelites stood before the Jordan River, it was the second time they faced a body of water as an obstacle. But before God parted the waters this time, His people had to get their feet wet. Only as they stepped in—only as they took that literal step of faith and trusted God—did He part the waters for them.

Like me, are you facing a river that looks impossible to cross? Well, I'm about to step into the water, trusting God, leaving the outcome to Him. Will you join me?

> *The river looks impassible . . .*
> *until you put your foot into the water.*

⇝ Five Minutes in the Word ↢

The priests will carry the Ark of the LORD, the Lord of all the earth. As soon as their feet touch the water, the flow of water will be cut off upstream, and the river will stand up like a wall.

Joshua 3:13

Trust in the LORD with all your heart and lean not on
your own understanding; in all your ways submit
to him, and he will make your paths straight.

Proverbs 3:5–6 NIV

I trust in your unfailing love; my heart rejoices in your salvation.
I will sing the LORD's praise, for he has been good to me.

Psalm 13:5–6 NIV

The LORD is my strength and my shield; my heart trusts
in him, and he helps me. My heart leaps for joy, and
with my song I praise him. The LORD is the strength of his
people, a fortress of salvation for his anointed one.

Psalm 28:7–8 NIV

My old self has been crucified with Christ. It is no longer I who
live, but Christ lives in me. So I live in this earthly body by trusting
in the Son of God, who loved me and gave himself for me.

Galatians 2:20

Time to Unload

I want you to imagine that it's Sunday morning and you're headed to church. You'd very nearly bailed. You've just been feeling so tired and discouraged lately. But you'd poured some coffee into a travel mug and headed out. The radio station is playing a familiar song . . . the hope-filled lyrics seem a bit out of reach. As you navigate the parking lot looking for those last few coveted spots, you watch families heading into the sanctuary, apparently carefree. You pick up your Bible and your purse, put on your best Sunday smile, and follow them.

Suddenly you feel this weight pulling on you. You look down and all the baggage from your life—the stuff you've been carrying inside for years—has become visible. And it's not easy to look at.

Fear

Shame

Insecurity

Disappointment

Regret

. . . and more. It's all there!

Panicking and not sure what to do, you look around and see that everyone else has baggage too. Everyone is weighed down by things they've been trying to bury for a long time. Then the service starts, so you just drag your stuff to your seat and sit down.

You hear a voice coming from the front of the church. It's not your pastor's voice; in fact, he is sitting at the edge of the platform, weighed down like everyone else. You realize that it's Jesus speaking.

Come to me, all of you who are weary and carry heavy burdens, and I will give you rest. Take my yoke upon you. Let me teach you, because I am humble and gentle at heart, and you will find rest for your souls. For my yoke is easy to bear, and the burden I give you is light. (Matthew 11:28–30)

These words are met with silence.

Then an older man stands up, drags his bag to the front, and leaves it there. A young couple does the same thing. More and more people begin to drag their baggage to the feet of Jesus and leave it there.

Will you go too?

Will you take Christ up on this amazing exchange?

You don't have to carry your baggage for one more minute!

> *Jesus' yoke is easy to bear
> and the burden is light.*

✒ Five Minutes in the Word ✒

*Come to Me, all who are weary and burdened, and I will
give you rest. Put My yoke upon your shoulders—it might
appear heavy at first, but it is perfectly fitted to your
curves. Learn from Me, for I am gentle and humble of
heart. When you are yoked to Me, your weary souls will
find rest. For My yoke is easy, and My burden is light.*
Matthew 11:28–30 *The Voice*

*Even youths shall faint and be weary, and young men shall fall exhausted; but they who wait for the L*ORD *shall renew their strength; they shall mount up with wings like eagles; they shall run and not be weary; they shall walk and not faint.*

Isaiah 40:30–31 ESV

Cast all your anxiety on him because he cares for you.

1 Peter 5:7 NIV

Since we are surrounded by such a huge crowd of witnesses to the life of faith, let us strip off every weight that slows us down, especially the sin that so easily trips us up. And let us run with endurance the race God has set before us.

Hebrews 12:1

The Facts Are In

Sometimes my husband Barry struggles when it comes to making a big purchase. When choosing a new phone, for instance, he can easily spend hours in a store looking at all the latest gadgets. I'm not like that. I decide what I want, then I go out, and I buy it. Done! Barry is more . . . thoughtful.

"I like the size of the screen on this one," he'll say.

I merely nod, because I know he's about to like the battery life on another. I simply walk along beside him like a nodding dog on a long, long walk.

"This one got great reviews," Barry mentions, "in addition to a couple really bad reviews.

"I wonder if this model comes in black.

"What kind of photos do you think I'd get on this one?

"Is this too big for my pocket?"

Finally, after I have sung through the entire score of

Handel's *Messiah* in my head, I'll inevitably say, "Will you just choose one?"

And Barry's response will be "But all the facts aren't in yet!"

I think we can be a bit like that in our relationship with God. We want to trust Him with everything, but we don't know what that might mean. We want to rest in God's peace, but we see so much trouble everywhere around us, both near and far. We want to forgive that woman in our small group who wounded or offended us and isn't the least bit sorry, but we're not sure we can really let it go.

If the jury were still out on the goodness, mercy, and grace of God, maybe you and I could be excused for not trusting God, resting in His peace, forgiving people, or doing any of the things He calls us to do. But all the facts we need to know about God are in:

God is sovereign.

God is love.

God is truth.

God is wisdom.

God is mercy.

God is for us.

God knows everything.

God is always with us.

With those facts in place, we have no reason not to act. We have no reason not to obey all that God commands. After all, those commands are for our good.

> *The facts are in: we have no*
> *excuse not to trust our God!*

⚜ Five Minutes in the Word ⚜

Commit your way to the LORD; trust in him, and he will act.
Psalm 37:5 ESV

Dear children, let's not merely say that we love each other;
let us show the truth by our actions. Our actions will
show that we belong to the truth, so we will be confident
when we stand before God. Even if we feel guilty, God is
greater than our feelings, and he knows everything.
1 John 3:18–20

Do all things without grumbling or disputing; so that you will prove yourselves to be blameless and innocent, children of God above reproach in the midst of a crooked and perverse generation, among whom you appear as lights in the world.

Philippians 2:14–15 NASB

I appeal to you therefore, brothers, by the mercies of God, to present your bodies as a living sacrifice, holy and acceptable to God, which is your spiritual worship. Do not be conformed to this world, but be transformed by the renewal of your mind, that by testing you may discern what is the will of God, what is good and acceptable and perfect.

Romans 12:1–2 ESV

If anyone is in Christ, he is a new creation. The old has passed away; behold, the new has come.

2 Corinthians 5:17 ESV

Who We Are in Christ

Sitting in the psychiatrist's office, I felt as if my pounding heart were going to burst out of my chest.

I had been admitted to the Northern Virginia Doctors Hospital the previous evening and was staying in the psychiatric wing. I have struggled with depression for a good part of my life. I never called it that, though. I just thought I had a melancholy personality and that sadness was simply woven into my DNA. But after months of feeling as if I were disappearing a little bit more every day, I had finally reached out to a friend for help, and this was where that journey had taken me.

"Who are you?" the doctor asked.

I thought it was a stupid question. I could see my name on the top of his yellow legal pad.

"I'm Sheila Walsh," I said.

"I know your name, Sheila," he responded kindly, "but who are you?"

A trick question! I thought. "I'm the co-host of *The 700 Club*."

"I didn't ask what you do, Sheila. I asked who you are."

That stumped me. "I don't know," I whispered.

"Well," he said. "That's why you're here."

My greatest nightmare growing up was that I would end up in a psych ward. My father was thirty-four when he escaped from the hospital where he was being held and took his own life. As I look back now, more than twenty years later, I can say with confidence that God's mercy led me to that psych ward.

When we are forced to face our greatest fears, we discover that Jesus is right there with us. I wrote in my journal that first night, "I never knew You lived so close to the floor." For a month I worked through the painful process of peeling back the layers I had created to protect myself. The opportunity to do so was a gift.

On the day I left, my doctor called out of his office window, "Sheila, who are you?"

I responded with everything in me, "I am Sheila Walsh, daughter of the King of kings!"

> **Sometimes God will take you to
> a prison to set you free.**

✦ Five Minutes in the Word ✦

Be strong and courageous. Do not be afraid or terrified
because of them, for the LORD your God goes with
you; he will never leave you nor forsake you.
Deuteronomy 31:6 NIV

I am sure that neither death nor life, nor angels nor rulers,
nor things present nor things to come, nor powers, nor height
nor depth, nor anything else in all creation, will be able to
separate us from the love of God in Christ Jesus our Lord.
Romans 8:38–39 ESV

Yet to all who did receive him, to those who believed in
his name, he gave the right to become children of God—
children born not of natural descent, nor of human
decision or a husband's will, but born of God.
John 1:12–13 NIV

Salvation is not a reward for the good things we have
done, so none of us can boast about it. For we are God's

masterpiece. He has created us anew in Christ Jesus, so we can do the good things he planned for us long ago.

Ephesians 2:9–10

It is God who enables us, along with you, to stand firm for Christ. He has commissioned us, and he has identified us as his own by placing the Holy Spirit in our hearts as the first installment that guarantees everything he has promised us.

2 Corinthians 1:21–22

No Stone Throwing Here!

The first cool breeze of fall was in the air when I boarded my flight from Dallas to San Antonio. It's such a short flight that by the time you have your Diet Coke in hand, it's time to give it back.

That evening I would be speaking to a group of women about moving from rage to restoration, from unforgiveness to freedom. That was a lot to cover in one forty-five-minute message, but the more I thought and prayed about what to say, the clearer it became . . . which explained the weight of my one checked bag.

"Are you checking any bags?" the man at the ticket counter had asked.

"Just one," I said. "This backpack."

He put on the appropriate luggage tag and then bent over to pick it up and move it onto the conveyer belt that would take it down to the baggage handlers.

The weight of the bag caught him off guard. "What do you have in here?" he asked. "Rocks?"

"As a matter of fact, yes," I replied.

He looked at me for a moment and then decided I was one of those women with whom one should keep conversation to a minimum.

I had six hundred and ten small river rocks tucked into my bag, a visual aid for the evening's message on forgiveness.

Forgiveness can be one of the hardest things to do. How do you forgive a spouse who cheats on you? How do you forgive someone who slanders your name? How do you forgive the drunk driver who takes the life of your child? How do you forgive someone who's not sorry? It's a deeply spiritual issue that I don't think we'll ever understand this side of heaven. However, forgiveness is not a matter of reason; it's a matter of obedience.

I carry a small stone with me everywhere I go. I have carried it for twenty-eight years, ever since God literally brought me to my knees over my reluctance to forgive someone who had devastated my life. When I finally surrendered to His command that I forgive that person, I realized that a stone was actually cutting into my knee. Now I carry that stone with me to cut into my heart and remind me of Jesus' words: "Let any one of you who is without sin be the first to throw a stone" (John 8:7 NIV).

> *Make a pledge to live a life of forgiveness—and find a stone to remind you of your promise.*

✦ Five Minutes in the Word ✦

"If you forgive those who sin against you, your heavenly Father will forgive you. But if you refuse to forgive others, your Father will not forgive your sins."

Matthew 6:14–15

Jesus bent down and started to write on the ground with his finger. When they kept on questioning him, he straightened up and said to them, "Let any one of you who is without sin be the first to throw a stone at her."

John 8:6–7 NIV

O Lord, you are so good, so ready to forgive, so full of unfailing love for all who ask for your help.

Psalm 86:5

*Peter came to Jesus and asked, "Lord, how many times
shall I forgive my brother or sister who sins against
me? Up to seven times?" Jesus answered, "I tell you,
not seven times, but seventy-seven times."*

Matthew 18:21–22 NIV

*Bear with each other and forgive one another if any of you has
a grievance against someone. Forgive as the Lord forgave you.*

Colossians 3:13 NIV

A Good Way to Start a Day

I don't trust hotel wake-up calls. Whether you will actually receive one when you ask seems to depend on the state of mind of the person entering your request. If he's just broken up with his girlfriend, for example, and her name happens to be Sheila, I'm either getting a call in the middle of the night or none at all. So I set my own alarm on my phone. I actually set two. The first is when it would be good to get up, and the second is when I'd jolly well better get up. I'm just not a morning person, so I like to ease into a day slowly.

I used to crawl out of bed, check that our son was up and in the shower, turn on the television to the morning news, and make myself a cup of coffee. It's not a bad way to start the day, but I've found a much better way. I realized that if the first thing I pay attention to is what's happening in our world, those images and words impact my view of the rest of the day. But if the Word of God is the first thing I give my heart and mind to, I see everything as under the control of my all-good, all-powerful, and all-loving heavenly Father. It's hardly surprising that this new start to my day has had a huge impact on my life.

The moment I awake, I say Psalm 143:8 (NIV) to myself—or, if Barry is already awake, I say it out loud. I repeat the verse several times. It's become a great way to start a day:

> *Let the morning bring me word of your unfailing love,*
>> My love will fall and fail, but God's love never will.

> *for I have placed my trust in you.*
>> The psalmist is very intentional here: trusting God is an act of the will.

> *Show me the way I should go,*
>> I pray, "Show me, Father, which way I should go today."

> *for to you I entrust my life.*
>> I say, "My life is Yours, Lord, and I trust You with everything."

Then I pray these simple words: "Good morning, Lord! I don't know where You are going today, but wherever You're going, I'm comin' with You!"

> *A good way to start the day every single day is to declare the Word of God and thank Him for it.*

❧ Five Minutes in the Word ☙

Let the morning bring me word of your unfailing love, for I have put my trust in you. Show me the way I should go, for to you I entrust my life.

Psalm 143:8 NIV

The steadfast love of the LORD never ceases; his mercies never come to an end; they are new every morning; great is your faithfulness.

Lamentations 3:22–23 ESV

Weeping may last through the night, but joy comes with the morning.

Psalm 30:5

It is good to proclaim your unfailing love in the morning, your faithfulness in the evening.

Psalm 92:2

Very early in the morning, while it was still dark, Jesus got up, left the house and went off to a solitary place, where he prayed.

Mark 1:35 NIV

Don't Drop It!

Many families hand down special keepsakes from those who've gone before them—a small piece of jewelry, a china plate, a favorite book. I have several such meaningful treasures, but not as many as my mum kept safely in a china cabinet. Among her collection, one vase in particular was clearly very special to her. Every spring she would take it out of the cabinet and wash it gently in a basin of warm soapy water before drying it and placing it back on display. Then she would say the same words I had heard her say during this ritual since I was a very small girl: "This vase has been passed down from generation to generation."

That vase fascinated me, so one day—even though I could see it just fine where it was—I decided I needed a closer look. I'd heard that the finest bone china is almost translucent when held up to the light. So I very carefully took the vase out of the cabinet and held it up to the light that was streaming through the window. "So beautiful," I said quietly to myself, but before the words had left my lips, the vase slipped through my fingers and shattered into a hundred pieces all over the living room carpet.

"I will need to leave home," I decided, but because I was only thirteen, my chance of survival wasn't promising. That meant I had no other option: I had to own it.

"Mum," I began, my heart in the pit of my stomach, "you know the vase that's been passed down from generation to generation?"

"Yes," she said.

"Well . . . this generation just dropped it!"

As silly as it sounds, that statement has stayed with me through the years, and more recently it has become a passionate prayer. I don't want us to be the generation that dropped it!

You and I are living in dark days. News from overseas becomes more troubling by the day, and within our own borders our basic rights as followers of Christ are being eroded bit by bit. But when we feel pressure to conform to ideas that are contrary to our faith, we can find ourselves tempted to sit quietly and wait for Christ to come rescue us.

I, however, don't want to be a silent observer of the demise of Christianity. I want to live my faith boldly—not merely with trite bumper-sticker phrases, T-shirt slogans, or easily dismissed clichés but with love, mercy, and grace that point people to Jesus.

So what can we do to stand strong in our faith and not drop the assignment God has given us? The greatest resource we have is God's power made available to us through both the Holy Spirit living within us and the written Word of God.

> *God's Word is sharper than any two-edged sword, but it's of no use if we can't remember where we put it.*

⟡ Five Minutes in the Word ⟡

*Who knows whether you have not come to
the kingdom for such a time as this?*
Esther 4:14 ESV

*The word of God is living and active, sharper than
any two-edged sword, piercing to the division of soul*

and of spirit, of joints and of marrow, and discerning
the thoughts and intentions of the heart.

Hebrews 4:12 ESV

Take up the whole armor of God, that you may be able to
withstand in the evil day, and having done all, to stand
firm. Stand therefore, having fastened on the belt of truth,
and having put on the breastplate of righteousness, and,
as shoes for your feet, having put on the readiness given by
the gospel of peace. In all circumstances take up the shield
of faith, with which you can extinguish all the flaming
darts of the evil one; and take the helmet of salvation,
and the sword of the Spirit, which is the word of God.

Ephesians 6:13–17 ESV

Your word is a lamp to guide my feet and a light for my path.

Psalm 119:105

Christi Is with You

D o you ever doubt that God is with you?

Do you look at the amount in your checking account and the pile of bills and wonder if God remembers where you live?

Do you find yourself in a dark place and wonder if you are lost?

When we allow circumstances to be the indicator of whether Christ is with us, we may start panicking when the sea starts getting rough.

Mark described an incident like that in chapter four of his gospel. The disciples were crossing the Sea of Galilee with Jesus and, tired from a day of teaching, He fell asleep. As the sea became rougher and rougher, the men began to panic. Waking Jesus, they asked Him, "Teacher, don't you care that we're going to drown?" (Mark 4:38). If you look back to verse 35, you'll see that they actually missed what Jesus said, which was, "Let's cross to the other side of the lake." He didn't say, "Let's get halfway across and drown." Jesus knew they would survive the stormy sea.

Sometimes we are just like those disciples, forgetting what we've been promised. The Christian life is a lot like that boat ride. Christ has told us where we're going, but sometimes in the midst of the journey we don't feel His presence and we can only see the overwhelming storms. Paul told his fellow believers, "I am certain that God, who began the good work within you, will continue his work until it is finally finished on the day when Christ Jesus returns" (Philippians 1:6). He didn't say that he hoped this would happen, or as long as nothing changed in the world it would be the case; he wrote, "I am certain." This man whose road to salvation involved a blinding encounter with the risen Christ reminds us that God was the One who began working in our lives, and He will be the one to complete that work.

If life feels a little rough right now, remember Christ's promises and that you are not alone, for He is in the boat with you.

> *Don't let a storm keep you from counting on what Jesus has told you.*

⋙ Five Minutes in the Word ⋘

As evening came, Jesus said to his disciples,
"Let's cross to the other side of the lake."
Mark 4:35

God has said, "I will never fail you. I will never abandon you."
Hebrews 13:5

"Teach these new disciples to obey all the commands
I have given you. And be sure of this: I am with
you always, even to the end of the age."
Matthew 28:20

God is my strength and power, and He makes my way perfect.
2 Samuel 22:33 NKJV

Since we are surrounded by so great a cloud of witnesses, let us
lay aside every weight, and the sin which so easily ensnares
us, and let us run with endurance the race that is set before us,
looking unto Jesus, the author and finisher of our faith, who for
the joy that was set before Him endured the cross, despising the
shame, and has sat down at the right hand of the throne of God.
Hebrews 12:1–2 NKJV

Welcomed by Royalty

I had practiced my curtsy for weeks, and I knew not to speak unless I was spoken to.

I'd been preparing to host a gala evening at the Royal Albert Hall in London, which Her Royal Highness Princess Anne would be attending. At the conclusion of the evening, those of us who had performed would be introduced to her, and I'd had the rules made very clear to me.

"Remember, the first time she addresses you, you must call her, Your Royal Highness," my palace coach began. "After that, you simply address her as Ma'am. Are we clear?"

We were clear!

The event went seamlessly until the receiving line. I was second in line, and my heart was racing. Princess Anne looked beautiful in a full-length green taffeta ball gown and dazzling emerald and diamond earrings. As she got closer, my mind went blank. Totally blank.

Do I call her "Your majesty"? No, that's for the Queen! I was in a total panic.

Suddenly Princess Anne was standing right in front of me, extending her lily-white hand. I blurted out the only English word I apparently still knew: "Hello!"

Over her shoulder I saw my palace instructor take a deep breath. *That's it! I'm going to be thrown into the Tower of London*, I thought.

But Princess Anne squeezed my hand and replied, "Hello to you too!"

Such grace. As thrilled as I was to meet a member of the royal family, it pales in comparison to what you and I are invited to do every moment of our lives. We have the privilege of entering the very throne room of Almighty God. Read that sentence again, because this truth may have become too familiar: We have the privilege of entering the very throne room of Almighty God. May our hearts beat a bit faster as we accept the invitation extended to us in Hebrews: "Let us come boldly to the throne of our gracious God. There we will receive his mercy, and we will find grace to help us when we need it most" (4:16). Jesus will graciously and lovingly accept us, tongue-tied or not!

> *Live every day knowing that you*
> *are a beloved child of the King of kings,*
> *always welcome to enter into His presence!*

ᨀ Five Minutes in the Word ᨀ

Yours, O Lᴏʀᴅ, is the greatness and the power and the
glory and the victory and the majesty, for all that is in the
heavens and in the earth is yours. Yours is the kingdom,
O Lᴏʀᴅ, and you are exalted as head above all.
1 Chronicles 29:11 ᴇsᴠ

All the kings of the earth shall give you thanks, O Lᴏʀᴅ, for
they have heard the words of your mouth, and they shall sing
of the ways of the Lᴏʀᴅ, for great is the glory of the Lᴏʀᴅ.
Psalm 138:4–5 ᴇsᴠ

Be exalted, Lᴏʀᴅ, in Your strength;
we will sing and praise Your might.
Psalm 21:13 ʜᴄsʙ

God has highly exalted [Jesus] and bestowed on him the name that is above every name, so that at the name of Jesus every knee should bow, in heaven and on earth and under the earth, and every tongue confess that Jesus Christ is Lord, to the glory of God the Father.

Philippians 2:9–11 ESV

A Bottle of Your Tears

W hen I opened the gift from my friend, I wasn't quite sure what it was. The small glass bottle was a beautiful cobalt blue, about two inches tall, covered in sliver filigree.

I thought it might be a perfume bottle, albeit a very small one, but her note explained that it was actually a tear bottle she'd found in an antique store in Israel. I did a little research and discovered that tear bottles were common in Rome and Egypt around the time of Christ. Mourners would collect their tears as they walked toward the graveyard to bury their loved one, a tangible indication of how much that person was loved. Sometimes women were even paid to follow the mourners and cry into such a vessel. Apparently the more anguish and tears produced, the more important and valued the deceased person was perceived to be. But legend has it those mourners-for-hire who cried the loudest and produced the most tears received the greatest compensation.

I treasure this little blue bottle because it reminds me of a profound spiritual truth David wrote about in Psalm 56, when he was at one of the lowest points of his life. David had been captured by his enemies in Gath (he had actually feigned insanity to survive), but he found comfort in the fact that God saw everything he was going through and caught every single tear he shed. I love David's confidence in the mercy and faithfulness of God even when he himself had not been faithful to the Holy One. David knew without a doubt that Almighty God never misses a moment, a tear, or a sigh from any of His children. Do you rest in that truth, or do you question that God loves you that much?

Do you ever feel alone? Have you ever thought, "No one on this earth understands the depth of my suffering"?

If you've taken a wrong turn in the road, are you expecting God to hold back His mercy until you get back on the straight and narrow?

That's not the God David knew; that's not the God of the Bible. We have a Father who keeps track of all our wanderings and catches every single tear we cry. When we begin to grasp the depth of that truth, we can say with confidence just as David did, "This I know: God is on my side!" (Psalm 56:9).

✧ Five Minutes in the Word ✧

You have kept count of my tossings; put my tears in your bottle. Are they not in your book?
Psalm 56:8 ESV

The LORD hears his people when they call to him for help. He rescues them from all their troubles. The LORD is close to the brokenhearted; he rescues those whose spirits are crushed.
Psalm 34:17–18

He heals the brokenhearted and bandages their wounds.
Psalm 147:3

Those who sow in tears shall reap with shouts of joy!
Psalm 126:5 ESV

"Blessed are those who mourn, for they shall be comforted."
Matthew 5:4 ESV

All Night Long

I have always loved movies. As a child I would've rather watched a movie than do almost anything else. There was one movie, however, I wasn't so sure about. I was twelve years old, and my mum was taking my sister Frances and me to see *The Ten Commandments*.

"I love the Bible, Mum, but I think this might be a bit of a yawn," I ventured.

She assured me that she'd heard great things about the special effects, and that all three of us would love it. I wasn't convinced.

We went to Green's Playhouse, the oldest movie theater in our town—which, to me, seemed appropriate. The theater had long velvet drapes that would swing open to reveal the screen. Well, they did most nights. That evening it took two men and a ladder to get those drapes open. When the movie finally began, I was, to my surprise, hooked.

I'll never forget how I felt when Charlton Heston—I mean Moses—held up his staff and the waters of the Red Sea parted . . . with much more ease than the drapes had. It only took seventeen seconds for the waters. (I know because I've gone back and timed it.) But that great scene in a movie is not an accurate picture of what Moses and the children of Israel experienced. Instead, as Moses himself reported, "The wind blew all that night, turning the seabed into dry land" (Exodus 14:21). *All night long!*

Have you ever prayed and wondered why it seemed like God wasn't doing anything? *What we can't see with human eyes is that God is working all night long.*

Have you cried for a child who has wandered off and shows no sign of ever turning back? *God is working all night long.*

Have you prayed for a job so you can support your family and, although you've poured out your heart, God seems deaf to your cries? *God is working all night long.*

Only God knows how long the night will be, but you can be absolutely certain that He is at work in the darkness. When you lay your head on your pillow tonight, cast your cares on Him and rest in the solid truth that He is working for your good!

> *When it appears there is no reason to hope,*
> *remember that God is working all night long.*

～ Five Minutes in the Word ～

Moses raised his hand over the sea, and the LORD opened up
a path through the water with a strong east wind. The wind
blew all that night, turning the seabed into dry land.

Exodus 14:21

Faith is the assurance of things hoped for,
the conviction of things not seen.

Hebrews 11:1 ESV

Your unfailing love, O LORD, is as vast as the heavens;
your faithfulness reaches beyond the clouds.

Psalm 36:5

Look around at the nations; look and be amazed! For I am doing something in your own day, something you wouldn't believe even if someone told you about it.

Habakkuk 1:5

If we look forward to something we don't yet have, we must wait patiently and confidently.

Romans 8:25

I Will Not Forget Your Word

Wandering through a used bookstore one day, I picked up a copy of *Pensées* (French for "thoughts") by Blaise Pascal. At the time I didn't know much about him, but for some reason I was drawn to this book. I soon learned that he was a French mathematician and physicist who had a dramatic encounter with God one night—it lasted two hours and changed his life forever. Pascal wrote about his experience on a piece of paper and sewed it into the lining of his coat. Whenever he changed what he was wearing, he transferred the paper so that he always had it with him. I don't know what the full text was, but I know it included, "Fire. God of Abraham, God of Isaac, God of Jacob," and it concluded with part of Psalm 119:16, "'I will not forget thy word.' Amen" (KJV).

As I thought about Pascal's lifelong commitment to carry with him a reminder of this holy experience, I wondered how you and I could incorporate something similar into our lives. What truth has He revealed to us, and how could we make an effort to remember it?

When I was baptized as a sixteen-year-old in my little Baptist church in Scotland, this verse was read as I entered the water:

> You did not choose me, but I chose you and appointed you that you should go and bear fruit and that your fruit should abide, so that whatever you ask the Father in my name, he may give it to you. (John 15:16 ESV)

Since that day, whenever I have questioned my ability or the effectiveness of my ministry, I have leaned on that truth. God chose me, He appointed me, and I can leave the rest to Him.

Perhaps a particular verse deeply impacted you at some point in your life. Maybe you chose a verse on a significant occasion like your baptism, wedding, or recommitment to Christ. Or when you were in a dark, difficult place, God gave you a verse that was a lifeline until morning came. If you don't really have a special verse, ask God to guide you to one. He wants you to walk through life mindful of Him and His love for you. And He can use His Word to make that happen.

❧ Five Minutes in the Word ❧

On my bed I remember you; I think of you
through the watches of the night.
Psalm 63:6 NIV

I recall all you have done, O LORD; I remember
your wonderful deeds of long ago.
Psalm 77:11

I have hidden your word in my heart
that I might not sin against you.
Psalm 119:11 NIV

Blessed are those whose ways are blameless, who
walk according to the law of the LORD. Blessed are

those who keep his statutes and seek him with all their heart—they do no wrong but follow his ways.

Psalm 119:1–3 NIV

"Make them holy by your truth; teach them your word, which is truth. Just as you sent me into the world, I am sending them into the world."

John 17:17–18 -

An Inescapable Love

I had just finished a day of Bible teaching and I was getting ready to head home when I noticed a young woman hovering in the back of the room as if she wasn't sure what to do next. I walked over to her, saying, "Thank you so much for coming."

"No, thank *you*!" she said. "And . . . I want to give you something." She handed me a bracelet with five rows of silver and gold beads.

"Thank you. It's lovely."

Her eyes filled with tears. "I've worn that bracelet for a long time to cover this," she said, pushing up the left sleeve of her sweater. "I tried to kill myself a few years ago. I've been so ashamed, so I wore the bracelet to cover my scar."

I hugged her tight. "Why are you giving this to me now?"

"Because I don't have to be ashamed anymore! I finally got it today. I don't have to be ashamed anymore!"

God had opened her heart to the radical grace of His gospel and the reality of His all-encompassing love. In Him, we can let go of whatever we have done or left undone, whatever we regret saying or wish we'd said. Once we are in a relationship with Christ Jesus, He wants us to move on, forgiven for our sin and free of any shame. But all too often sticky shame makes more sense to us. We have *done* something bad, and we feel as if we *are* bad. We forget that on the cross Jesus dealt such shame a deathblow so that you and I can be free.

When Paul wrote to believers in Rome, his heart was ablaze with God's overwhelming love. As he spelled out its lavish depth and breadth, he spoke to those hearers who believed that whatever they had done was too much for God to forgive. Hear with your heart Paul's bold and confident declaration in Romans 8:38–39: absolutely nothing can separate you from God's love. You are loved and you are forgiven. Go in peace.

> *There's no fine print: absolutely nothing can separate you from God's love.*

～ Five Minutes in the Word ～

I am sure that neither death nor life, nor angels nor rulers,
nor things present nor things to come, nor powers, nor height
nor depth, nor anything else in all creation, will be able to
separate us from the love of God in Christ Jesus our Lord.
Romans 8:38–39 ESV

How precious is your steadfast love, O God! The children
of mankind take refuge in the shadow of your wings.
Psalm 36:7 ESV

Have mercy on me, O God, according to your unfailing love;
according to your great compassion blot out my transgressions.
Psalm 51:1 NIV

I pray that out of [the Father's] glorious riches he may
strengthen you with power through his Spirit in your inner
being, so that Christ may dwell in your hearts through faith.
And I pray that you, being rooted and established in love,

may have power, together with all the Lord's holy people, to
grasp how wide and long and high and deep is the love of
Christ, and to know this love that surpasses knowledge—that
you may be filled to the measure of all the fullness of God.

Ephesians 3:16–19 NIV

See what great love the Father has lavished on us,
that we should be called children of God!

1 John 3:1 NIV

Enduring When We
Want to Quit

T his is too hard, Mom! I can't do this."

My heart ached for my son. His junior year of high school had brought on a ridiculous amount of homework, research, and writing. I don't remember having half as much work to do when I was his age.

I looked into my son's big brown eyes. "Christian, God has given you an amazing brain. You are smart, and you've worked hard for your good grades. Now you just have to dig a little deeper. When you are applying to colleges next year, you'll see the fruit of the seeds you plant this year."

"That seems like a long way off," he said with a wry smile as I headed out to buy him one of his favorite (disgusting) fast-food beverages.

It's hard to keep going when the finish line seems

far away. It's even harder when no one is cheering you on or buying you peculiar blue coconut beverages to refuel you. Furthermore, perseverance has little curb appeal in our culture of microwave speeds and an attitude of entitlement. We want what we want when we want it, but God's Word has a lot to say about continuing on when you want to quit.

I've spent a lot of time on the road for over thirty years, and although I love what I do, every now and then I've thought, "This is too hard. I'm done." Whenever I begin to think like that, I immediately go back to the following passage from the book of Hebrews, a passage that speaks so powerfully of the perseverance of Christ Jesus, our greatest example of all:

> Since we are surrounded by such a great cloud of witnesses, let us throw off everything that hinders and the sin that so easily entangles. And let us run with perseverance the race marked out for us, fixing our eyes on Jesus, the pioneer and perfecter of faith. For the joy set before him he endured the cross, scorning its shame, and sat down at the right hand of the throne of God. Consider him who endured such opposition from sinners, so that you will not grow weary and lose heart. (Hebrews 12:1–3 NIV)

"Consider him"! Think about what Jesus persevered through—and that He did so out of love for you and me. Thinking of all Christ has done for us can help us take a deep breath and keep on running!

> *Consider what Jesus has done for you whenever you grow weary in what you are doing for Him.*

～ Five Minutes in the Word ～

We can rejoice, too, when we run into problems and trials, for we know that they help us develop endurance. And endurance develops strength of character, and character strengthens our confident hope of salvation. And this hope will not lead to disappointment.

Romans 5:3–5

Give thanks to the LORD, for he is good; his love endures forever.

1 Chronicles 16:34 NIV

"Do not work for food that spoils, but for food that endures to eternal life, which the Son of Man will give you. For on him God the Father has placed his seal of approval."

John 6:27 NIV

"Sin will be rampant everywhere, and the love of many will grow cold. But the one who endures to the end will be saved."

Matthew 24:12–13

God blesses those who patiently endure testing and temptation. Afterward they will receive the crown of life that God has promised to those who love him.

James 1:12

Amazing Grace

L et's call her 'Amazing Grace,'" Christian suggested.

"That's a great name for a parrot," I replied. "Why did you choose it?"

"Because this time, at the funeral, she'll know we're talking about her."

Every time we bury one of our son's critters, I am expected to sing at least two verses of the classic hymn "Amazing Grace." Fish get two verses, hamsters usually get the whole thing, and upon the untimely demise of our cat, Thomas O'Malley, Christian wanted me to hire bagpipes! (I used a CD instead.)

The line Christian loves most is "I once was lost but now I'm found." And I totally get that. We all want to know that we belong and that if we ever wander off, someone will come looking for us.

One of Jesus' best known stories is about a boy who

did wander off—the prodigal son. It's a story that would have shocked Jesus' audience. For a son to demand his share of his inheritance while his father was still alive was an outrageous insult. In that culture fathers were to be held in high regard. To ask for his father's money and then to waste it on reckless partying showed that the son had absolutely no respect for his dad. The story also included what would have been a chilling picture for Christ's audience: a Jewish boy caring for pigs! He had become the unclean living among the unclean.

The most offensive part of the story, however, would have been not the ungrateful son, but the grace-filled father. "When [the son] was still a great way off, his father saw him and had compassion, and ran and fell on his neck and kissed him" (Luke 15:20 NKJV).

You and I probably smile as we imagine the joy-filled father running toward his boy, but for a Jewish audience this picture was unthinkable. A wealthy, respected father, one who stood in the shadow of Abraham himself, would never pick up his robes and run, especially to the person who had brought such disgrace to his family. This story was profoundly offensive—and it still is. The grace of God deeply offends those of us who think there is even one cell of our being that deserves the love of God more than someone else does.

✺ Five Minutes in the Word ✺

"While [his son] was still a long way off, his father saw him and felt compassion, and ran and embraced him and kissed him."
Luke 15:20 ESV

God proves His own love for us in that while we were still sinners, Christ died for us!
Romans 5:8 HCSB

By grace you have been saved through faith. And this is not your own doing; it is the gift of God, not a result of works, so that no one may boast.
Ephesians 2:8–9 ESV

From [the Son's] fullness we have all received, grace upon grace.
John 1:16 ESV

I do not account my life of any value nor as precious to myself, if only I may finish my course and the ministry that I received from the Lord Jesus, to testify to the gospel of the grace of God.

Acts 20:24 ESV

Driven to Her Knees

One of the greatest heartaches a woman can experience is the inability to have a child of her own. Not every woman longs for motherhood, but for women who do and who month after month are disappointed they have not conceived, the pain they feel is cruel and unrelenting.

On top of that heartache, a woman in Old Testament times was burdened by the common belief that childlessness was a curse, a sign that God was angry with her, as well as by the sense that she had failed her husband. After all, every man longs for a son, an heir, someone to carry on the family name.

Played out against this backdrop is one of the most moving stories I've ever read, the story of a woman we meet in 1 Samuel 1. Hannah was one of Elkanah's two wives. This is how the author introduced her: "Peninnah had children, but Hannah did not" (1 Samuel 1:2). Nothing more needed to be said.

Adding to Hannah's pain was the cruelty of the other wife: "Peninnah would taunt Hannah and make fun of her because the LORD had kept her from having children. Year after year it was the same" (1:6–7). That kind of ongoing pain changes a person. It either draws her closer to the heart of God, who understands suffering, or it makes her question His love or even His very existence.

What did Hannah choose to do in her darkest night? This heartbroken woman knew where to take her pain: "Hannah got up and went to pray" (v. 9). And she prayed with such passion that Eli, the priest, thought she was drunk. Hannah wasn't drunk; she was desperate. She told Eli, "I was pouring out my heart to the LORD" (v. 15).

Hannah could have become bitter toward Peninnah, toward Elkinah, and even toward God, but instead she cried out to Him in her pain. May we do the same.

> *Let your pain drive you to your knees,*
> *for there you will find your greatest strength.*

∽ひ Five Minutes in the Word ⌒Ɔ⌐

*[The Lord] gives strength to the weary and increases the power
of the weak. Even youths grow tired and weary, and young men
stumble and fall; but those who hope in the Lord will renew
their strength. They will soar on wings like eagles; they will
run and not grow weary, they will walk and not be faint.*
Isaiah 40:29–31 NIV

*In returning and rest you shall be saved;
in quietness and trust shall be your strength.*
Isaiah 30:15 ESV

*The Lord is near to the brokenhearted
and saves the crushed in spirit.*
Psalm 34:18 ESV

Cast all your anxiety on [God] because he cares for you.
1 Peter 5:7 NIV

Wisdom for Life's Crossroads

The moment Christian hit his senior year in high school, the brochures started arriving. Those from small colleges listed a few majors. Others rivaled *War and Peace* in length. The most memorable one came from a pharmaceutical school: it was shaped like a large pill bottle complete with warnings about potential side effects:

May result in a successful career

Complications could include high income

Can lead to a career with job security

This creative marketing approach underscored how pivotal such crossroads in life can be: Which college should I attend? Should we buy a new house? What job offer makes the most sense? Is this the right person to marry?

King Solomon, who wrote most of the book of Proverbs, was known for one thing above all others: "God gave Solomon very great wisdom and understanding, and knowledge as vast as the sands of the seashore. In fact, his

wisdom exceeded that of all the wise men of the East and the wise men of Egypt" (1 Kings 4:29–30). In light of Solomon's "very great wisdom," I find comfort in his statement that when we trust God rather than simply relying on what makes sense to us and when we honestly want to do God's will, He will indeed show us the path to take.

Life for the believer is not a tightrope walk off a threatening precipice and across a deep canyon. Instead, we can journey confidently and step-by-step with our loving Father as a guide. After all, He wants to show us His will even more than we want to see it.

> *Your Good Shepherd longs to make His will known to you. Just ask.*

⮐ Five Minutes in the Word ⮑

Trust in the LORD with all your heart; do not depend on your own understanding. Seek his will in all you do, and he will show you which path to take.

Proverbs 3:5–6

*Lead me in the right path, O L*ORD*, or my enemies will
conquer me. Make your way plain for me to follow.*
Psalm 5:8

*Show me the right path, O L*ORD*; point out the road for me to follow.*
Psalm 25:4

*May the God of hope fill you with all joy and peace
as you trust in him, so that you may overflow
with hope by the power of the Holy Spirit.*
Romans 15:13 NIV

*In Scripture it says: "See, I lay a stone in Zion, a
chosen and precious cornerstone, and the one who
trusts in him will never be put to shame."*
1 Peter 2:6 NIV

Worship the King

Christmas cards depicting the night Christ was born typically include Mary, Joseph, the baby Jesus, shepherds, a smattering of farm animals, and the Magi, who we refer to as the "three wise men." Those travelers from the east, however, didn't actually come until later—probably not until Jesus was a toddler. (Matthew 2:11 tells us they visited the baby in a home, not a stable.) They followed the star of Bethlehem and traveled about nine hundred miles, most likely from Persia, modern day Iran. Why?

They may have been familiar with this prophecy of Balaam, who lived near Persia: "I see him, but not now; I behold him, but not near: a star shall come out of Jacob, and a scepter shall rise out of Israel" (Numbers 24:17 ESV). They were educated enough to read the signs, and they knew that this little boy was the promised King. They had said to King Herod, "Where is the newborn king of the Jews? . . . We have come to worship him" (Matthew 2:2).

We can't give Christ gold, frankincense, and myrrh the way the Magi did, but we can give Him the greatest gift the wise men offered: the gift of their worship. Whether we kneel with heads bowed low or we stand with our arms raised high, we declare that He alone is worthy of praise. Worship is not only a precious gift to God; it also changes us. Worship puts us in a right position with Christ and adjusts our perspective. It fills our hearts with love for Him and encourages our faith like nothing else can.

No wonder the wise men made such an effort to be where Jesus was. What an honor it is to worship the King, and what a joy it is to love Him!

O come, let us adore Him, Christ the Lord!

✦ Five Minutes in the Word ✦

*"Where is the newborn king of the Jews? We saw his
star as it rose, and we have come to worship him."*
Matthew 2:2

Because of your unfailing love, I can enter your house;
I will worship at your Temple with deepest awe.

Psalm 5:7

Who may worship in your sanctuary, LORD? Who may enter
your presence on your holy hill? Those who lead blameless lives
and do what is right, speaking the truth from sincere hearts.

Psalm 15:1–2

So the women hurried away from the tomb, afraid yet
filled with joy, and ran to tell his disciples. Suddenly
Jesus met them. "Greetings," he said. They came
to him, clasped his feet and worshiped him.

Matthew 28:8–9 NIV

I urge you, brothers and sisters, in view of God's mercy, to
offer your bodies as a living sacrifice, holy and pleasing
to God—this is your true and proper worship.

Romans 12:1 NIV

The Best Thing We Can Do

Jimmy never missed a church service. I knew him when I was a teenager growing up in Scotland, and I can still remember how he prayed at our Tuesday night prayer meetings. Every single week he prayed for his wife, asking God to give her the desire to know Jesus. The beautiful northern brogue with which Jimmy spoke of his passion for Jesus left an indelible mark on my heart. His wife was a lovely woman, but she had no desire to have anything to do with Jimmy's church or his God. But he kept on praying. He never stopped praying. And then he died.

I wonder if God told Jimmy when He welcomed him home that his prayers had been answered. At Jimmy's memorial service, his wife finally bowed her knee to the Savior he had served all his life. There wasn't a dry eye in the church that day as we celebrated the fruit of a prayer warrior who completely trusted God's promises and never stopped praying.

Sometimes when we pray for a person and our prayers

seem to make no difference, we can feel like giving up. The Enemy would love for us to believe the lie that our prayers make no difference at all. And that's exactly what it is: a lie. In Luke 18, Jesus told about a widow who would not quit asking a judge for help even when he continued to ignore her. According to Luke, "Jesus told his disciples [this] parable to show them that they should always pray and not give up" (18:1 NIV).

I've heard people say, "The only thing left to do is pray." But it's not the *only* thing left to do; it's always the best thing we can do!

> *Prayer is not the last resort; it's the first and most effective line of attack.*

⊰ᑺ Five Minutes in the Word ᑺ⊱

There was also a prophetess, Anna, a daughter of Phanuel, of the tribe of Asher. She was well along in years, having lived with her husband seven years after her marriage, and was a widow for 84 years. She did not leave the temple complex, serving God night and day with fasting and prayers.

Luke 2:36–37 HCSB

Truly God has listened; he has attended to the voice of
my prayer. Blessed be God, because he has not rejected
my prayer or removed his steadfast love from me!
Psalm 66:19–20 ESV

[The LORD] will listen to the prayers of the destitute. He will not
reject their pleas. Let this be recorded for future generations,
so that a people not yet born will praise the LORD.
Psalm 102:17–18

"Whatever you ask in prayer, you will receive, if you have faith."
Matthew 21:22 ESV

Rejoice in hope, be patient in tribulation, be constant in prayer.
Romans 12:12 ESV

Peace in Jesus' Presence

I find it fascinating that we know very little about most of the men and women we meet in the pages of the Bible. Rather than an entire history, there are a few brief verses or, at best, a handful of chapters that tell how an encounter with the living God changed their lives and their eternal destinies.

I've always wanted to know more, for instance, about the so-called Gadarene demoniac we meet in Mark 5. Jesus and His closest friends encountered this wild man after a stormy nighttime crossing of the Sea of Galilee. Jesus' friends were fishermen, experienced in navigating the sudden storms that blew up out of nowhere, but something about that night was particularly disturbing. My theory is that demonic elements were stirring up the sea, for when Jesus stood to calm the sea, He said, "Peace! Be still!" (Mark 4:39 ESV). In the Greek, this is the very phrase Jesus used earlier to rebuke a demon (Mark 1:25). I'm convinced that evil itself was trying to keep Jesus away from delivering one poor, tormented man from his demons.

This man's life was as stormy as the sea Jesus had calmed. The evil spirit within him enabled him to break any chains people used to try to subdue him. The demoniac wandered through the hill country and its burial caves, "howling and cutting himself with sharp stones" (Mark 5:5). But the minute Jesus stepped onto the shore, the demoniac ran to Jesus and fell at His feet. This man had probably never heard of Jesus, but the demons within him immediately recognized "Jesus, Son of the Most High God" (v. 7). I imagine the man thinking, *I don't know who You are, but those who torment me are afraid of You!*

You can read the whole story in Mark 5, but in the end Christ commanded the demons to leave the man and enter the pigs that were feeding on the hillside. The herd immediately ran off the edge of the cliff and into the water. It was a chaotic scene—except for one place. When the local townspeople heard about the uproar, they hurried to go see "the man who had been possessed by the legion of demons, sitting there, dressed and in his right mind; and they were afraid" (Mark 5:15 NIV).

I love that the stories of Jesus calming the storm and Jesus freeing the demoniac are back-to-back. Whether a storm is raging in outside circumstances or inside your heart, when Jesus speaks to it, that storm has to obey. As we see in this pair of stories, Jesus brings peace to storms and chaos, internal as well as external.

> *The most peaceful place to be is with Jesus.*

⸻ Five Minutes in the Word ⸻

[Jesus] got up, rebuked the wind and said to the waves, "Quiet! Be still!" Then the wind died down and it was completely calm.

Mark 4:39 NIV

"Peace I leave with you; my peace I give you. I do not give to you as the world gives. Do not let your hearts be troubled and do not be afraid."

John 14:27 NIV

"In this world you will have trouble. But take heart! I have overcome the world."

John 16:33 NIV

*"Abide in me, and I in you. As the branch cannot
bear fruit by itself, unless it abides in the vine,
neither can you, unless you abide in me."*

John 15:4 ESV

*He who dwells in the shelter of the Most High will abide
in the shadow of the Almighty. I will say to the LORD, "My
refuge and my fortress, my God, in whom I trust."*

Psalm 91:1–2 ESV

Waiting on God's Green Light

For some very good reasons, I didn't learn to drive until I was twenty-seven years old and living in the US. I grew up in Scotland, and my mum was a widow. There simply wasn't enough money for all three of us children to get driving lessons. My sister, Frances, got them as a gift from a church friend because she was the eldest. My brother, Stephen, got driving lessons because he was a guy. And I . . . took the bus!

When I moved to California, though, I realized that if I didn't learn to drive, I would be staying home until Christ returned. The first few lessons were a bit dodgy. In fact, they seemed to require the instructor to have me pull over so he could get a cup of coffee and a couple aspirin. But I got the hang of it. Soon the only issue we had was traffic lights. I could tell when they were about to turn green—I just kind of felt it in my bones—but that special skill of mine did not sit well with the instructor.

"You have to wait until you get a green light!" he noted, quite forcefully.

That's a good phrase to apply to our spiritual life as well. When we're at a crossroads, we are wise to wait until we get a green light before we move ahead. But it can be tempting to run ahead of God, can't it? Sometimes God just seems to be taking too long to get back to us!

Whenever I have tried to move ahead of God's perfect timing, I've always ended up regretting it. When there is no clear green light, God wants us to wait. David himself—the man after God's own heart—encouraged us to be patient: "Wait on the LORD; be of good courage, and He shall strengthen your heart; wait, I say, on the LORD!" (Psalm 27:14 NKJV).

Only God knows the road that lies ahead. So when we're not sure what to do, let's choose to wait on the Lord in faith and do nothing. As J. I. Packer wrote, "When action is needed, light will come." He must have had the same driving instructor I had.

God's green light is always worth waiting for.

✏ Five Minutes in the Word ✏

*Faith is the assurance of things you have hoped for, the
absolute conviction that there are realities you've never seen.*

Hebrews 11:1 *The Voice*

*Listen to my voice in the morning, LORD. Each morning
I bring my requests to you and wait expectantly.*

Psalm 5:3

*You are my strength; I wait for you to rescue
me, for you, O God, are my fortress.*

Psalm 59:9

*Hope that is seen is not hope, because who hopes
for what he sees? But if we hope for what we do not
see, we eagerly wait for it with patience.*

Romans 8:24–25 HCSB

*I waited patiently for the LORD; he inclined
to me and heard my cry.*

Psalm 40:1 ESV

God Is for Us

What do you think a person's life looks like when God is clearly with him or her? What are some signs of a favored life? Let me suggest a few things:

We get the job when we apply for it.

Our marriage gets better and better as we fall more in love each day.

Our children honor God with their lives and never turn their backs on Him.

We are in unshakably good shape financially.

You get the idea. Surely if God is with us, life should work out well. But our Old Testament friend Joseph has a different story to tell.

We first meet Joseph in Genesis 37 when he's just seventeen years old—and his ten older brothers hate him with a passion. Joseph was his dad's favorite (Jacob didn't even try to hide that fact), and Joseph was spoiled

(oblivious to what an obnoxious little brother he was). So when the ten saw a chance to get rid of the pest, they took it. The brothers threw Joseph into an empty well to let him die, but they ended up selling him to slave traders heading for Egypt. When the traders sold Joseph to Potiphar, a captain of Pharaoh's guard, we see this phrase for the first time: "The LORD was with Joseph" (39:2). Really? Being sold into slavery wasn't a sign that God had left him?

Next the wife of his boss tried to seduce Joseph. When he resisted her advances, she accused him of rape, and Joseph was thrown into prison. Again we see the phrase, "The LORD was with Joseph" (39:21). If the Lord really were with Joseph, wouldn't you expect Him to defend Joseph when he did the right thing by rejecting Potiphar's wife?

Well, Joseph did well in jail and was put in charge of the other prisoners. After several years, he was given the opportunity to interpret dreams for two of Pharaoh's former servants who had also been thrown into prison. When one of the servants was about to be released, Joseph had a simple enough request: "When you get out of here, will you please mention to Pharaoh that I didn't do what I was imprisoned for?" (my paraphrase). Not a tough assignment, but the man forgot, so Joseph spent two more years in prison.

Long story short, when Joseph was finally released and found himself face-to-face with the brothers who had betrayed him, he made this remarkable statement: "You intended to harm me, but God intended it all for good" (50:20).

May we—like Joseph—trust that God does that same thing today. No matter what is happening in our lives, our sovereign Redeemer is at work for our good.

> *The Lord is always with you*
> *and always at work for your good.*

✥ Five Minutes in the Word ✥

The keeper of the prison paid no attention to anything
that was in Joseph's charge, because the LORD was with
him. And whatever he did, the LORD made it succeed.

Genesis 39:23 ESV

As I was with Moses, so I will be with you; I
will never leave you nor forsake you.

Joshua 1:5 NIV

*Keep your lives free from the love of money and be
content with what you have, because God has said,
"Never will I leave you; never will I forsake you."*
Hebrews 13:5 NIV

*"Go therefore and make disciples of all nations, baptizing
them in the name of the Father and of the Son and of the Holy
Spirit, teaching them to observe all that I have commanded
you. And behold, I am with you always, to the end of the age."*
Matthew 28:19–20 ESV

*I will see Your face in righteousness; when I awake,
I will be satisfied with Your presence.*
Psalm 17:15 HCSB

Marked for Life Eternal

Sometimes the start of a new year isn't really all that happy. Case in point: I ended the old year with the flu, which was followed by pneumonia that lasted for several weeks into the new year. Then one morning as I got out of bed, my right leg gave way underneath me. As the day went on, I regained use of it, but the pain was intense. My doctor referred me to a pain specialist who gave me an anesthetic and tried three times to block the pain for me. And three times it didn't work. Finally he sent me to a neurosurgeon because surgery was the only remaining option. The surgeon explained that he'd have to go in through my back to remove one disc in my spinal column and through the front to get the other.

"You'll have a six-inch vertical scar on both sides," he told me. "Your bikini days might be over."

I informed him that since I was raised Scottish Baptist, they were over when I hit three!

The surgery went well, and by God's grace I made a great recovery. As the scars began to heal, I saw that my body was now marked in an interesting way. I'd had surgery the previous year to remove a benign tumor, so I already had a horizontal three-inch scar on my tummy. When the final dressings were removed, I saw that I bore the perfect image of a cross.

Strange as it might seem, I really like it. I now have a 24/7 reminder that I follow a Savior who chose to be marked for you and for me. Jesus chose the scars that have healed us. He walked in our shoes and felt our pain. Because He loves us so much, He allowed Himself to be brutally beaten, to have the flesh torn from His back, to have His body pierced for our transgressions. In Him we can be forgiven of our sins and we are free to be in relationship with our heavenly and holy Father.

Hallelujah, what a Savior!

> *Jesus chose the scars that gained us freedom from sin as well as life eternal.*

❧ Five Minutes in the Word ❧

He heals the brokenhearted and binds up their wounds.

Psalm 147:3 ESV

He was pierced for our transgressions; he was crushed
for our iniquities; upon him was the chastisement that
brought us peace, and with his wounds we are healed.

Isaiah 53:5 ESV

[The soldiers] stripped [Jesus] and put a scarlet robe on him,
and twisting together a crown of thorns, they put it on his head
and put a reed in his right hand. And kneeling before him, they
mocked him, saying, "Hail, King of the Jews!" And they spit on
him and took the reed and struck him on the head. And when
they had mocked him, they stripped him of the robe and put
his own clothes on him and led him away to crucify him.

Matthew 27:28–31 ESV

He was oppressed and afflicted, yet he did not open his mouth; he was led like a lamb to the slaughter, and as a sheep before its shearers is silent, so he did not open his mouth.

Isaiah 53:7 NIV

The next day John saw Jesus coming toward him and said, "Look, the Lamb of God, who takes away the sin of the world!"

John 1:29 NIV

Worshipping with Nothing Hidden

It was a very unusual thing Jesus did that day, but according to the text, He was on assignment from His Father. As the apostle John put it, "[Jesus] had to go through Samaria" (John 4:4). In the Greek, the phrase *had to* didn't mean that this was the only option available for travel, but rather that Jesus felt compelled to take this road. After all, a route through Samaria was not a road any Jew would normally choose. Considering the Samaritans half-breeds, the Jews avoided them at all costs. Jesus, however, was on a rescue mission. He was being led by the Spirit.

If you are familiar with the story, you'll remember that the woman Jesus met at the well in Samaria had been married five times and was now living with a man who wasn't her husband. How had she ended up in such a situation? No young woman ever dreams that her life will turn out like that. Well, I have a theory.

I'm sure this woman was in love with the first man she married, but if she weren't able to have children, he probably divorced her pretty quickly. And in those days, young divorced women were not well taken care of, so she would have been glad to receive another proposal. Who knows what happened in that marriage? Or the next time? Or the next? By the time she encountered Jesus, this woman was simply grateful for a roof over her head, even if there were no ring on her finger.

When Jesus asked her to go get her husband, she told Him she didn't have a husband. Jesus said to her, "You have had five husbands, and the man you now have is not your husband" (John 4:18 NIV). The woman was stunned that this Jewish rabbi knew about her private life. Assuming that Jesus must be a prophet, she tried to engage Him in a discussion about the correct place to worship. But Jesus cut to the very heart of worship and said, "God is Spirit, and his worshipers must worship in the Spirit and in truth" (v. 24 NIV). Here, the word *truth* means "nothing hidden." And that is the kind of worship you and I are called to today.

Jesus already knows our secrets and our shame, but He still invites us to come—just as we are—into the light of His presence and receive His love. When we finally understand that God knows everything about us and that He nevertheless loves us deeply, that realization will change our lives.

A footnote to the story: the Samaritan woman became the first missionary to her village. "Come, see a man who told me everything I ever did. Could this be the Messiah?" (4:29 NIV).

> *Worship the One who knows you completely,*
> *knowing you are covered in His steadfast love.*

⁓ Five Minutes in the Word ⁓

"God is spirit, and his worshipers must
worship in the Spirit and in truth."
John 4:24 NIV

"You will know the truth, and the truth will set you free."
John 8:32

Lead me by your truth and teach me, for you are the God who saves me. All day long I put my hope in you.

Psalm 25:5

Unfailing love and truth have met together. Righteousness and peace have kissed! Truth springs up from the earth, and righteousness smiles down from heaven.

Psalm 85:10–11

If we claim to have fellowship with him and yet walk in the darkness, we lie and do not live out the truth. But if we walk in the light, as he is in the light, we have fellowship with one another, and the blood of Jesus, his Son, purifies us from all sin.

1 John 1:6–7 NIV

Broken Beyond Repair

I spent an amazing year of my life working in a home for emotionally disturbed teenagers, some of the most battered and broken among us. The life of one boy in particular—I'll call him Sam—was a nightmare.

From Sunday night until Friday afternoon, Sam was in my care, but if he chose to, he could go home for the weekend. His profound loyalty to his dysfunctional family shocked me. His dad was a violent drunk, and his mom was a small woman who had been battered into silence. Sam would come back to our unit on Sunday nights covered with bruises, insisting that he'd fallen down the stairs or off his bike—and there was absolutely nothing I could do. His violent outbursts at school had landed him in our care, but he still had the right to return to the home that had shattered his concept of love.

I wept for Sam on my knees.

I wrestled with God over the life of this boy.

I begged God to intervene.

How, I asked the Lord, *can I tell Sam that nothing could ever separate him from Your love when curses and fists tell him otherwise?*

When my year at the home ended, I told Sam that I would continue to pray for him. I also told him that sometimes the most powerful prayer is a single word: "Jesus!"

Several years later I was back in the area speaking. At the end of the evening, I was gathering my stuff in the dressing room when there was a knock at the door. It was Sam. With tears running down his cheeks, he told me how often he had prayed that simple prayer and that now Jesus was the strength of his life. Such is the unlimited love of our God!

As Jesus said, "The Son of Man came to seek and to save the lost" (Luke 19:10 NIV). The word for *lost* used here is *apollymi*. It means "devastated; ruined; broken beyond repair."

Do you know someone—or are you that someone—who has been crushed by life events? Know that we can never be too wounded to be healed by Jesus.

> *Jesus came for those of us who seem broken beyond repair.*

‍ Five Minutes in the Word ‍

"The Son of Man came to seek and to save the lost."
Luke 19:10 NIV

*"If a man has a hundred sheep and one of them gets lost, what
will he do? Won't he leave the ninety-nine others in the wilderness
and go to search for the one that is lost until he finds it? And when
he has found it, he will joyfully carry it home on his shoulders."*
Luke 15:4–5

*[The Pharisees] said to [Jesus'] disciples, "Why does
your teacher eat with tax collectors and sinners?" But
when [Jesus] heard it, he said, "Those who are well have
no need of a physician, but those who are sick."*
Matthew 9:11–12 ESV

*Here is a trustworthy saying that deserves full acceptance: Christ
Jesus came into the world to save sinners—of whom I am the worst.*
1 Timothy 1:15 NIV

I am convinced that neither death nor life, neither angels nor demons, neither the present nor the future, nor any powers, neither height nor depth, nor anything else in all creation, will be able to separate us from the love of God that is in Christ Jesus our Lord.

Romans 8:38–39 NIV

A Holy Life

One day when I was in the mall, I asked a random group of teenagers what the word *holiness* means. My question was met with silence until one girl said, "It's something to do with religion."

Another girl added, "I think that's the name of the church at the end of our street."

These days *holiness* is not a popular word, even in the churches at the end of our streets.

Several days later I asked the same question to a group of teenagers at my church.

"It means you don't drink or do drugs," one boy said.

"Or sex," another added. "It means no sex."

The Old Testament Hebrew word for *holy* is *qodesh*. It means "apartness, set-apartness, sacredness." In the New Testament, the word for *holy* is *hagios*, and it means "set apart, revered, sacred, and worthy of veneration." *Holiness* also suggests behavior that is acceptable to God, but there is so much

more to it. After all, Christianity is not simply a behavior modification program. Christianity is a call to a personal, radical, sold-out relationship with Jesus, and the result is a whole new way of living every moment of every day. And one aspect of this new way of living is holiness.

But you and I can't become holy by ourselves, as the apostle Paul acknowledged: "I have been crucified with Christ. It is no longer I who live, but Christ who lives in me" (Galatians 2:20 ESV). To be a disciple of Jesus Christ requires nothing less than death to our own selfish nature so that the life and the love of Christ can live in us. In other words, every time my will is in conflict with God's will, I—by the power of the Holy Spirit—drag my will into line with God's.

Bottom line, our world's greatest need is not for one more church building, but for believers filled with the love and power of God who shine brightly in this dark and ever-darkening planet.

I love what evangelist and teacher D. L. Moody said: "A holy life will produce the deepest impression. Lighthouses blow no horns; they only shine."

Let your light shine!

⪼⪻ Five Minutes in the Word ⪼⪻

*Again Jesus spoke to [the people], saying, "I am the
light of the world. Whoever follows me will not walk
in darkness, but will have the light of life."*

John 8:12 ESV

*"Let your light shine before others, so that they may see your
good works and give glory to your Father who is in heaven."*

Matthew 5:16 ESV

*The light shines in the darkness, and the
darkness has not overcome it.*

John 1:5 ESV

*The way of the righteous is like the first gleam of dawn,
which shines ever brighter until the full light of day.*

Proverbs 4:18

*Feed the hungry, and help those in trouble. Then
your light will shine out from the darkness, and the
darkness around you will be as bright as noon.*

Isaiah 58:10

A Chosen One

I stepped into the elevator and right away I knew that something was going on. The floor was covered in glitter and sequins, and the aroma of cheap hairspray hung in the air. When the elevator stopped, two little girls and their moms got on. The girls were wearing what can only be described as pageant dresses, and they had enough hair between them to make a banquet hall full of bald men envious.

Having put the pieces together, I asked, "Is the pageant over?"

"No," one of the moms replied. "We still have crowning!"

I dropped my briefcase off in my room and decided to join the festivities. I don't think I should have been allowed in the ballroom, but everyone was so preoccupied with what was about to happen, no one stopped me. I watched these little girls—the final five who were competing for the title—step up on stage to be judged. When the winner was announced, I watched the other four, and the expressions on their faces were absolutely heartbreaking. The message those four had heard was "You are *not* the prettiest. You are *not* the best."

And we get messages like that throughout our lives. We live in a culture that values things that have very little—if anything—to do with our heart or our character and everything to do with our appearance. We need to remember that God never sees us that way!

When God looks at you, He sees the beauty of His Son who has washed you whiter than snow.

When God looks at you, He sees His chosen daughter.

When God looks at you, He gazes with love . . . and love alone.

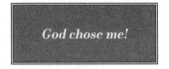

God chose me!

✦ Five Minutes in the Word ✦

You are a chosen generation, a royal priesthood, a holy nation, [God's] own special people, that you may proclaim the praises of Him who called you out of darkness into His marvelous light.

1 Peter 2:9 NKJV

[The LORD] brought out His people with joy,
His chosen ones with gladness.
Psalm 105:43 NKJV

God has chosen the foolish things of the world to put to
shame the wise, and God has chosen the weak things of
the world to put to shame the things which are mighty.
1 Corinthians 1:27 NKJV

My beloved speaks and says to me: "Arise, my
love, my beautiful one, and come away."
Song of Solomon 2:10 ESV

Those who were not my people I will call "my people,"
and her who was not beloved I will call "beloved."
Romans 9:25 ESV

How Much Do You
Think You're Worth?

When Christian was a senior in high school, Barry and I decided to put our house on the market. I'd felt for some time that it was more house than we needed, and now, with the prospect of our son leaving for college, we agreed to find something a bit smaller.

We met with a realtor to go over the details. My first question was "How do you decide on the right price for a home?" She said that several factors helped determine the cost, but the bottom line was this: "Your home is worth what someone is willing to pay for it." I love that!

So let's use this solid bit of real estate wisdom to establish once and for all that our lives are worth whatever Someone is willing to pay for it.

Think about that for a moment. Jesus Christ, the sinless Lamb of God, willingly left the glory of heaven to come to earth where He would be misunderstood, betrayed, and brutally executed—and He did that because He has determined that our lives are worth that cost! We forget way too easily the incredible value Christ places on us.

Perhaps it's easy for you to believe this truth about Jesus' love for other people, but you struggle to believe it for yourself. If that's the case, then place your name in the beloved text of John 3:16—"For God so loved _____ that He gave His only begotten Son, that [if he/she] believes in Him _____ should not perish but have everlasting life" (NKJV).

If you look only to a husband, children, a career, or friends, you can never get an accurate read of your true value. The reality is that Almighty God alone determines that, and He decided before you were even born that you are worth the life of His only Son. You are a treasured daughter of the King of kings.

> *Jesus paid with His life the price*
> *He believes you are worth.*

❧ Five Minutes in the Word ❧

*"God so loved the world that He gave His only
begotten Son, that whoever believes in Him should
not perish but have everlasting life."*

John 3:16 NKJV

*You formed my inward parts; you knitted me together in
my mother's womb. I praise you, for I am fearfully and
wonderfully made. Wonderful are your works; my soul
knows it very well. My frame was not hidden from you,
when I was being made in secret, intricately woven in the
depths of the earth. Your eyes saw my unformed substance;
in your book were written, every one of them, the days that
were formed for me, when as yet there was none of them.*

Psalm 139:13–16 ESV

*God shows his love for us in that while we
were still sinners, Christ died for us.*

Romans 5:8 ESV

If anyone is in Christ, he is a new creation. The old has passed away; behold, the new has come.

2 Corinthians 5:17 ESV

To all who did receive [Jesus], to those who believed in his name, [God] gave the right to become children of God.

John 1:12 NIV

Taking Time to Grieve

Years ago Barry and I—and our Ragdoll cat, Abigail—made the move from Nashville to Orange County, California. We estimated that the cross-country drive would take thirty hours, so we decided to drive ten a day, spending only two nights in a hotel as we headed west.

Abigail began the trip in a crate in the backseat, but that only lasted for about two hours. That was all of her pitiful howling that Barry and I could take, so I let her out. She settled down on the back window ledge, and peace was restored.

When it began to get dark, we decided to stop at the first hotel we saw. Not knowing what their pet policy was and not wanting to ask, Barry suggested that I shove Abigail up the front of my sweater as we walked through the lobby to our room.

Let me just say that if her tail wasn't sticking out, her head was! If I managed to hide her head, suddenly I was

dealing with the tail and a paw. I just could not keep that cat hidden quietly under my sweater.

Well, I've discovered in my own life that grief and pain are like that. We can try to bury them, we can do our best to push them far beneath the surface, but they don't cooperate. They wrestle back.

When one of my friends experienced a significant and painful loss, she told a grief counselor that she simply didn't have time to work through her pain. The counselor said, "You can grieve now and let your emotions out, or you can let those powerful feelings slowly leak out for the rest of your life."

At times we can be afraid to feel the full extent of our pain for fear it will overwhelm us. But hear God's promise: "The LORD is close to the brokenhearted; he rescues those whose spirits are crushed" (Psalm 34:18). Furthermore, God has given us the Holy Spirit to be our Comforter, but we can only be comforted when we acknowledge that we are hurting.

So when we're hurting, let's choose to give ourselves time to grieve. We don't need to be afraid to let the waves of sorrow hit us. Oh, we may feel pain like we've never felt before, but God won't let us deal with that pain alone. God is with us. Always.

> *When our pain is the greatest, God is the closest.*

ᏩᎨ Five Minutes in the Word ᏩᎨ

Why is your heart sad?
1 Samuel 1:8 ESV

Sorrow is better than laughter,
for sadness has a refining influence on us.
Ecclesiastes 7:3

Do not be afraid, for I have ransomed you. I have called you
by name; you are mine. When you go through deep waters, I
will be with you. When you go through rivers of difficulty, you
will not drown. When you walk through the fire of oppression,
you will not be burned up; the flames will not consume you.
Isaiah 43:1–2

From the ends of the earth I call to you, I call as my heart grows faint; lead me to the rock that is higher than I. For you have been my refuge, a strong tower against the foe.

Psalm 61:2–3 NIV

We are afflicted in every way, but not crushed; perplexed, but not driven to despair; persecuted, but not forsaken; struck down, but not destroyed; always carrying in the body the death of Jesus, so that the life of Jesus may also be manifested in our bodies.

2 Corinthians 4:8–10 ESV

Healing for a Broken Heart

It's the most loaded question a wife can ask her husband: "How do I look?"

There's no right answer. If he says, "I love that dress!" she'll immediately wonder what was wrong with the one she had on before.

If he says, "I'm not a huge fan of that skirt," she'll hear, "I'm not a huge fan of you" or "What were you thinking when you bought that?" or "It looks like you swallowed our children!"

I discovered that the tiebreaker in this family standoff can be a teenage son. He has no dog in the hunt, but if he has an opinion (doubtful), he will definitely say what he really thinks.

Now, I'll give you a little backstory. I'm Scottish born, so the allure of a bargain runs deep in my DNA. I don't wait for mere sales. I wait for the "Offer us anything and it's yours!" markdown. For example, I bought a pair of jeans that had

been reduced from $1,000 (unthinkable!) to $54. This was either the bargain of the year or a waste of $54—I couldn't decide which.

So I waited until Barry and Christian were relaxing in the den before I made my entrance. Barry saw me coming in and said nothing. I cleared my throat. Christian looked up with a look of . . . wonder in his eyes.

"Okay," I bravely began. "Tell me the truth. What do you think?"

Silence.

"I mean it. Tell me the absolute truth. It won't hurt my feelings!"

Christian sighed, "The eighties called, Mom. They want their jeans back."

Okay, so sometimes the truth might hurt a little bit, but when we are talking about our relationship with Christ, the truth He speaks to us about His love for us can mean deep healing.

Remember the story in Mark 5 when the woman who fell at Jesus' feet didn't have to tell Him the whole truth about herself? She'd already touched Him and been fully healed. All she had to do at that point was slip away, wait for seven days, and, with an offering, present herself to the priest. Then she would be declared whole and free to rejoin society.

But when Jesus asked a question—"Who touched me?"—she didn't just slip away. Despite the big, bustling crowd, the busy day, and the fact that many people had touched Him, this woman knew Jesus was talking to her. This was a key moment: would she play it safe or would she choose to be all in? Making her choice, she fell at Jesus' feet and told Him her story, the truth about her disease, her healing, her faith in His goodness and power.

Have you ever talked to Jesus like that? Have you ever told Him—out loud—your story and held nothing back? When we do so, the response from heaven can change our lives . . . just as Jesus' kind and loving response to the once-bleeding woman changed hers: "Daughter, your faith has made you well. Go in peace" (Mark 5:34).

> *Facing the truth of our own story might break our heart, but telling it to Jesus could heal it.*

⮞◌ Five Minutes in the Word ◌⮜

The woman, knowing what had happened to her, came and fell at [Jesus'] feet and, trembling with fear, told him the whole truth.

Mark 5:33 NIV

Lᴏʀᴅ, who may dwell in your sacred tent? Who may live on your
holy mountain? The one whose walk is blameless, who does
what is righteous, who speaks the truth from their heart.

Psalm 15:1–2 NIV

Behold, you delight in truth in the inward being,
and you teach me wisdom in the secret heart.

Psalm 51:6 ESV

The Lᴏʀᴅ is close to all who call on him,
yes, to all who call on him in truth.

Psalm 145:18

"God is Spirit, so those who worship him
must worship in spirit and in truth."

John 4:24

Do You Want to Get Well?

My connecting flight had been late, so I was the last to board my flight home. I'd had to run from Gate A4 to Gate B15, so by the time I flopped into my seat, I could hardly breathe. I quickly fastened my seatbelt, and we were off. The woman sitting beside me asked if I'd like a piece of gum, and before I could answer, she started to laugh.

"Is my hair all over the place?" I asked.

"Well, it is, but that's not why I'm laughing," she said. "Look what I'm reading."

She held up a copy of my book *The Shelter of God's Promises*.

"Thank you," I said. "What made you pick up that book?"

"Because I'm stuck," she said. "And I've been stuck for years."

"Okay," I said. "Try to tell me the story of your life in five minutes."

"It'll take a lot longer than that," she said.

"I'll listen to the long version, too, but first give it to me in five."

I have found that this exercise effectively reveals what we consider the most significant moments in our lives. In her five-minute version all this dear woman talked about was the husband who had left her years ago. The impact and betrayal had been devastating, but she had chosen to define her whole life according to that one event. That's why she was stuck.

Jesus met many people who were stuck. The man lying by the pool of Bethesda for thirty-eight years is an example. And what did Jesus say to him? Jesus' question may have seemed quite insensitive: "Would you like to get well?" (John 5:6). The importance of the question, however, outweighed the risk of appearing insensitive. To get well—to get unstuck—we have to be willing to let go of what *was* and to embrace what *is*.

If I asked you to tell me the story of your life in five minutes, what would you say? What would be the main events, the turning points, and the tough places? I'd like to encourage you to take a few minutes sometime today and try this exercise. When we tell our story in five minutes and then pay attention to what we have focused on, then we can—by God's grace—take steps to get unstuck.

Life brings moments that devastate, but we have a Savior who came to heal and to give us hope.

⌒ Five Minutes in the Word ⌒

When Jesus saw him and knew he had been ill for a long time, he asked him, "Would you like to get well?"
John 5:6

Jesus told him, "Stand up, pick up your mat, and walk!"
John 5:8

Then your salvation will come like the dawn, and your wounds will quickly heal. Your godliness will lead you forward, and the glory of the LORD will protect you from behind. Then when you call, the LORD will answer. "Yes, I am here," he will quickly reply.
Isaiah 58:8–9

He was pierced for our transgressions; he was crushed
for our iniquities; the punishment that brought us peace
was on him, and by his wounds we are healed.

Isaiah 53:5 NIV

[The bleeding woman] said to herself, "If I only
touch [Jesus'] cloak, I will be healed."

Matthew 9:21 NIV

Let the Shepherd Carry You

The first time I took Christian to visit his Scottish family, he was two years old. Although he was happy to meet everyone, he was definitely more interested in the sheep.

Scotland is a land of sheep. If you drive down the west coast, you'll pass field after field of very white sheep. I've always been fascinated by sheep and how the image of Christ as our Good Shepherd appears throughout Scripture. I've learned much about Jesus' tender care of His flock by studying sheep, especially those that shepherds call "bummer lambs."

Bummer lambs have, for one reason or another, been rejected by their mothers. If, for instance, a ewe has triplets and only enough milk for two, she will turn away the third. If a ewe is old or sick, she might reject a lamb. To preserve the life of those unwanted bummer lambs, the shepherd has to take the lamb into his home and bottle-feed it. He'll hold the lamb to keep it warm and so that it can hear a heartbeat. When the lamb is strong enough to return to the flock, the shepherd takes it there. And in the morning or at the end of the day, when the shepherd calls to the sheep, the first ones to run to him are the bummer lambs because they know his voice so well.

When my life fell apart and I was hospitalized for depression, I thought my life was over. I had no idea that any kind of gift could come from this brokenness. But Jesus is close to us when we are broken, and He carries us for as long as we need Him to. It's not that He loves us more than the sheep that happen to be stronger; it's just that we are privileged to experience His tender love in an unforgettable and very personal way that makes us confident about His great love for us. Jesus rescued me, a bummer lamb, and nursed me back to strength and health. A special reassurance of His great love for me resulted. What began as the bad news became the best news of all: Jesus truly does love us bummer lambs.

If you find yourself in a broken place, let the Shepherd carry you. Join the fields of bummer lambs like me—and countless others—who, when the world went quiet, learned to recognize the life-giving voice of the Shepherd.

> *When we are lost or broken, we can come to know God's love in a more profound way.*

⚬⚬ Five Minutes in the Word ⚬⚬

"I am the good shepherd. The good shepherd gives His life for the sheep."

John 10:11 NKJV

"[The shepherd] calls his own sheep by name and leads them out. After he has gathered his own flock, he walks ahead of them, and they follow him because they know his voice."

John 10:3–4

"I am the good shepherd; I know my own sheep, and they know me, just as my Father knows me and I know the Father. So I sacrifice my life for the sheep."

John 10:14–15

The LORD is close to the brokenhearted
and saves those who are crushed in spirit.
Psalm 34:18 NIV

He heals the brokenhearted and binds up their wounds.
Psalm 147:3 NIV

"It Is Finished"

E very word Jesus spoke was pregnant with meaning,
perhaps none more so than His final cry from the
cross: "It is finished!" (John 19:30). When we understand
more about the Jewish faith in Jesus' day, we can start to
grasp how significant this statement was and how stag-
gering the events surrounding his death were.

Consider, for instance, that even as Jesus uttered these
haunting words, Passover lambs were being slaughtered in
the temple, barely a mile away from Calvary. According to
the Old Testament sacrificial system, the blood of lambs
was spilled at Passover: it was the faithful Jews' offering as
an atonement for their sins. On this remarkable Passover,
though, this longstanding system was replaced by the
once-and-for-all sacrificial death of Jesus. The spilled
blood of the perfect, spotless Lamb of God paid for the sins
of all humanity, from eternity past to eternity future.

The gospel writer Matthew reported that as Jesus spoke

these final words, the curtain in the temple separating the Holy Place from the Holy of Holies was ripped cleanly in two from top to bottom. No man could have torn the curtain from the top down—it was about sixty feet high and four inches thick! This curtain had served as the "Do Not Enter" sign for the place where, just once a year, on the Day of Atonement, the high priest would offer blood sacrifices for the sins of the people. In that moment when Christ said, "It is finished," the curtain separating a holy God from sinful men and women was removed forever!

Can you imagine what that must have been like for the priests who were in the temple that day? They must have realized that only one hand could have done this, the hand of God.

When Jesus said, "*It* is finished," He declared that He had done what God had sent Him to do: die on behalf of sinful humanity. Because Jesus died and rose again, our sins are forgiven and we are washed clean. So anytime the Enemy tries to make us feel guilty or causes us to doubt whether we have actually been forgiven, let's quote our Savior and remind the deceiver: "It is finished!"

> *Our sins are forgiven once and for all. It is finished!*

ᴄ Five Minutes in the Word ᴐ

When Jesus had received the sour wine, He said, "It is finished!" And bowing His head, He gave up His spirit.
John 19:30 NKJV

Then Jesus shouted out again, and he released his spirit. At that moment the curtain in the sanctuary of the Temple was torn in two, from top to bottom.
Matthew 27:50–51

Come now, let us reason together, says the LORD: though your sins are like scarlet, they shall be as white as snow; though they are red like crimson, they shall become like wool.
Isaiah 1:18 ESV

The accuser of our brothers and sisters has been thrown down to earth—the one who accuses them before our God day and night. And they have defeated him by the blood of the Lamb and by their testimony.
Revelation 12:10–11

The next day John saw Jesus coming toward him and said,
"Look! The Lamb of God who takes away the sin of the world!"

John 1:29

The Family of God

Last year my son, Christian, and I drove deep into the heart of Texas to buy a Yorkshire terrier puppy. We'd checked out the breeder's website, and the puppies and parents were adorable black-and-tan balls of energy. As we pulled into the long gravel driveway, dogs of every breed, size, and shape—plus two peacocks, five goats, and a rooster—ran out to greet us.

We knocked on the front door and Wanda the breeder escorted us into a small room off the kitchen. "Wait here," she said, "and I'll bring the puppies out." Soon Christian and I were on the floor laughing as seven tiny, barking bundles of joy crawled all over us. After Christian chose the one he wanted, we headed home to Dallas with four-pound, twelve-week-old Maggie in her crate.

Well, she grew and grew—and even today she still appears committed to growing. I asked our vet what she thought about the lineage of our rapidly expanding Yorkie,

and she said, "Her mom may have been a Yorkie but something else got in there!" Whatever breed she is, Maggie is part of our family and she is loved.

It's my fervent prayer that we as the church would be able to say the same thing about everyone in the family of God. I believe that we are on the brink of a true revival, and some of the people who will come pouring through our doors will not look like the perfectly turned-out Sunday school crowd. When Paul wrote to the church in Rome, he addressed the religious and social stereotypes of his day directly. Some of the wealthiest people of the day had come to Christ—and so had their servants. Many Jews had found their faith completed in Christ but struggled with non-Jews being accepted into the very same spiritual family. Paul's passionate plea to Christians was that they learn that in Christ we are one family.

I believe that for too long we have found comfort and safety in being around those who look like they share a spiritual mother with us, when the reality is, the ground at the foot of the cross is even. Everyone you will meet today has two things in common with you: they have been made in the image of God, and they need Jesus.

Will you join me in praying that we will see others through the eyes of Christ with love and acceptance, just as He has received each one of us?

⚬ Five Minutes in the Word ⚬

*The human body has many parts, but the many parts
make up one whole body. So it is with the body of Christ.
Some of us are Jews, some are Gentiles, some are slaves,
and some are free. But we have all been baptized into one
body by one Spirit, and we all share the same Spirit.*
1 Corinthians 12:12–13

*If we are living in the light, as God is in the light,
then we have fellowship with each other, and the
blood of Jesus, his Son, cleanses us from all sin.*
1 John 1:7

*Whenever we have the opportunity, we should do good to
everyone—especially to those in the family of faith.*
Galatians 6:10

So we, though many, are one body in Christ, and individually members one of another.

Romans 12:5 ESV

God Has Come to Us

When I was a child, a distant aunt insisted on knitting me a new hat every Christmas. I tried to be grateful, but they were truly atrocious creations. The worst one was purple and yellow with great wool loops all over it. (I was convinced that if a bird flew low enough over my head, I was going wherever it was going.) Making these gifts harder to accept graciously was the fact that this aunt bought my brother whatever the latest toy was. When I asked my mother about this glaring discrepancy, she said, "Her gifts say a lot, Sheila. She spends a long time knitting those hats." Mum was right about gifts saying a lot, and I'll leave it at that.

The gifts that the Magi brought to Jesus spoke volumes too. Myrrh was used as an embalming spice in those days; it pointed to the death Jesus would die on our behalf, the payment for our sins. The gold was so valuable that many commentators believe Joseph used it to cover

the costs of traveling to Egypt, following the angel's command and keeping Jesus safe after Herod ordered the slaughter of all baby boys.

But I find the frankincense most amazing. It's mentioned in the book of Exodus when God reveals His design for the tabernacle—the place where He would be present with His people. Exodus 30:22–38 has specific instructions about an incense that was to be offered to the Lord: "Never use this formula to make this incense for yourselves. It is reserved for the LORD, and you must treat it as holy. Anyone who makes incense like this for personal use will be cut off from the community" (vv. 37–38).

This incense was to be burned in front of the Ark of the Covenant at the place where God would meet the high priest. Clearly, this incense signified the presence of God with His people. And what exactly was in this special incense? God instructed them to gather fragrant spices and "mix these fragrant spices with pure frankincense" (v. 34).

As the Magi placed their gifts before the Christ Child, the message was loud and clear: God has come to us!

> *In this very moment, God offers you the gift of His presence.*

◦❖◦ Five Minutes in the Word ◦❖◦

When [the wise men] saw the star, they rejoiced exceedingly
with great joy. And going into the house they saw the
child with Mary his mother, and they fell down and
worshiped him. Then, opening their treasures, they
offered him gifts, gold and frankincense and myrrh.

Matthew 2:10–11 ESV

For to us a child is born, to us a son is given; and
the government shall be upon his shoulder, and his
name shall be called, Wonderful Counselor, Mighty
God, Everlasting Father, Prince of Peace.

Isaiah 9:6 ESV

The angel said to [the shepherds], "Fear not, for behold, I bring you
good news of great joy that will be for all the people. For unto you is
born this day in the city of David a Savior, who is Christ the Lord."

Luke 2:10–11 ESV

The people walking in darkness have seen a great light; on those living in the land of deep darkness a light has dawned.

Isaiah 9:2 NIV

Look! The virgin will conceive a child! She will give birth to a son, and they will call him Immanuel, which means "God is with us."

Matthew 1:23

The Power of God's Word

It's one of the most powerful scenes from Jesus' life, and it happened just before His public ministry began.

After John baptized Jesus, the Holy Spirit led Him into the wilderness where, for forty days, the devil tempted Him to do *what* God wanted Him to do but not the *way* God wanted Him to. Interestingly, the only reason we have this story is because Jesus must have told His closest friends what happened. And it was an important story for Jesus to share because in that experience, He set the pattern for His ministry and for us.

Clearly Jesus understood the great power that was at His disposal. Of course Satan won't tempt us to turn a stone into bread or throw ourselves off the roof of our church building; he knows our limitations. Jesus knew He could make rocks into food and expect angels to catch his fall, but he chose the way of suffering—the way of the cross—over the path of instant glory and fame.

The temptations Jesus faced fell into three categories:

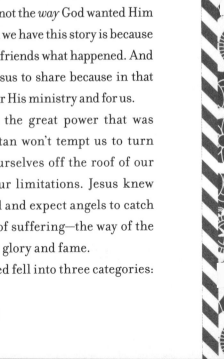

Provide for Yourself. Material things make people happy!

Choose the power without the cross. A little compromise will save You so much pain!

Show Yourself to be the Messiah. If You do, You'll immediately have loyal followers.

Jesus underwent forty days of this relentless onslaught. His temptations were far more intense than any you or I will ever face, and the stakes were much higher. If Jesus had weakened and succumbed, we would all be lost in our sins, for Jesus would no longer have been the sinless Lamb of God. But even in His physical weakness, Jesus stood firm against the Enemy. The gospel writer Luke told us one source of His strength: Jesus responded to each temptation with statements of truth directly from the Word of God. The Son of God used the Word of God against the Enemy of God. And why would we mere humans do anything else?

When Paul wrote to believers in Ephesus, he described the spiritual armor available to them. Every piece but one is for defense, and that exception is God's Word. Paul called believers to "take the sword of the Spirit, which is the word of God" (Ephesians 6:17).

We all face temptations, and as the days get darker, the fight for our loyalties and for our very souls will become fiercer. But God has provided all that we need—the powerful truth of Scripture!

⚕ Five Minutes in the Word ⚕

*Then the devil said to [Jesus], "If you are the Son of God, tell
this stone to become a loaf of bread." But Jesus told him, "No!
The Scriptures say, 'People do not live by bread alone.'"*
Luke 4:3–4

*May the praise of God be in [the] mouths [of the faithful]
and a double-edged sword in their hands.*
Psalm 149:6 NIV

*The word of God is living and active, sharper than any two-edged
sword, piercing to the division of soul and of spirit, of joints and of
marrow, and discerning the thoughts and intentions of the heart.*
Hebrews 4:12 ESV

All Scripture is inspired by God and is useful to teach us what is true and to make us realize what is wrong in our lives. It corrects us when we are wrong and teaches us to do what is right. God uses it to prepare and equip his people to do every good work.

2 Timothy 3:16–17

For as the rain and the snow come down from heaven and do not return there but water the earth, making it bring forth and sprout, giving seed to the sower and bread to the eater, so shall my word be that goes out from my mouth; it shall not return to me empty, but it shall accomplish that which I purpose, and shall succeed in the thing for which I sent it.

Isaiah 55:10–11 ESV

Alive and Victorious!

W hich person, alive or dead, would you choose to talk with over coffee, and why?"

The question came from a group of ladies whose church conference I would be speaking at in a few months. They thought it would be fun to include some trivia in the program. The first couple of questions were easy. Chocolate or chips? *Chocolate!* Favorite animated movie? *Finding Nemo.* But I had to think about that third question for a bit, and I ended up settling on Mary Magdalene. She especially understood the power and reality of evil, and so her joy in Christ's victory over sin, suffering, and death must have run deep. It would be an honor to see her example of faith, love, and worship up close.

The gospel writers tell us that Mary Magdalene was possessed by seven demons (Mark 16:9; Luke 8:2), and in Scripture the number *seven* denotes "completion." Apparently this poor woman had been totally possessed

189

by evil until the day she came face-to-face with Jesus Christ and He set her free.

Then she watched her Lord and Savior suffer—battered and bleeding, carrying His cross up a hill where He would be brutally executed. She saw His lifeblood drip onto the very ground He had spoken into existence. After Christ had taken his last breath, Mary followed Nicodemus and Joseph as they carried Jesus' body to a garden tomb. Early the next morning, when it was still dark, she went back to that tomb—and the stone had been rolled away. Mary ran to Peter and John and told them that Christ's body was missing. The two men went and saw it for themselves: the tomb was empty! After Peter and John left, Mary looked inside the tomb a second time and saw two angels. They asked her, "Dear woman, why are you crying?" (John 20:13).

In light of all that had happened the previous two days—and really, throughout much of her life—that question might have seemed odd. Mary could have given a long list of reasons to be crying. And if Jesus' body had still been there on that Easter Sunday morning, then we all would have a reason to cry. But Jesus *wasn't* there! He was—and is—alive!

Many people have studied the lives of great leaders, but only those of us whose allegiance is to Christ alone serve a risen, victorious Savior. He conquered sin and death, and we who name Him Savior and Lord will do the same. Like Mary, we now have reason to rejoice instead of cry. Whatever you are facing right now, remember the empty tomb: Jesus is alive, and because of that, we win in the end!

> *Our Lord is not in the tomb—He is alive!*

✎ Five Minutes in the Word ✎

I have told you all this so that you may have peace in me.
Here on earth you will have many trials and sorrows.
But take heart, because I have overcome the world.
John 16:33

The light shines in the darkness, and the
darkness has not overcome it.
John 1:5 ESV

He isn't here! He is risen from the dead, just as he said
would happen. Come, see where his body was lying.
Matthew 28:6

During the forty days after he suffered and died, he
appeared to the apostles from time to time, and he
proved to them in many ways that he was actually alive.
And he talked to them about the Kingdom of God.

Acts 1:3